Studies of Italy

Edward A. Freeman

Alpha Editions

This edition published in 2024

ISBN : 9789364731058

Design and Setting By
Alpha Editions
www.alphaedis.com
Email - info@alphaedis.com

As per information held with us this book is in Public Domain.
This book is a reproduction of an important historical work. Alpha Editions uses the best technology to reproduce historical work in the same manner it was first published to preserve its original nature. Any marks or number seen are left intentionally to preserve its true form.

CONTENTS

Arezzo. ....- 1 -

Cortona. ....- 4 -

Perugia. ....- 8 -

The Volumnian Tomb. ....- 11 -

Præ-Franciscan Assisi. ....- 15 -

Spello. ....- 19 -

Veii. ....- 22 -

Fidenæ. ....- 25 -

Antemnæ. ....- 28 -

Ostia. ....- 31 -

The Alban Mount. ....- 35 -

Cori. ....- 40 -

Norba. ....- 44 -

Segni. ....- 48 -

Iter ad Brundisium. ....- 52 -

I. Anagni. ....- 53 -

II. Ferentino..- 59 -

III. Alatri. ....- 66 -

IV. From Alatri to Capua. ....- 71 -

V. A Church by the Camp of Hannibal............- 75 -

VI. A Glimpse of Samnium. ....- 80 -

VII. Benevento..- 84 -

VIII. Norman Buildings in Apulia. ....- 89 -

IX. Bari. ....- 93 -

AREZZO.

The city of Mæcenas, and of a whole crowd of famous men of later times, shows no outward signs of being much frequented by travellers. There is some difficulty there in getting so much as an Italian newspaper, and, though excellent photographs have been taken of some of the chief buildings, they must be sought for at Florence; they are not to be bought at Arezzo. Yet the old Etruscan city has many attractions, among them surely the singular cleanness of its streets, and, above all, that clear and pure air which is thought to have had something to do with nourishing the genius of so many of its citizens in so many different ways. Perhaps, on the whole, Arezzo does not suffer from not having yet put on the cosmopolitan character of some of its neighbours. And if the city does not, either as Arretium or as Arezzo, stand forth in the first rank of Italian cities, still it has a long history under both forms of its name. If, again, its buildings do not rank with those of Pisa or Lucca, still there is quite enough both in the general aspect of the city, and in some particular objects within its walls, to claim a day or two's sojourn from any one who is not eager to rush from Florence to Rome as fast as the so-called express train can carry him.

Arezzo, as to its physical site, holds a middle position between cities which sit perched on a high hill-top like Fiesole, and cities which, like Florence, lie flat or nearly so on the banks of a great river. It has its river, if we may give that name to the mere brook which presently loses itself in the Chiana, as the Chiana soon loses itself in the Arno. The river too has a bridge, but both river and bridge have to be sought for; they form no important points in the general aspect of the city. The bridge at Arezzo is not one of those to which we instinctively go the first thing to take a general view of the city as a whole. The hill is a more real thing, as any one will say who climbs some of its steeper streets. Still it is one of those hills which seem to borrow height and steepness from the fact of being built upon. If it were covered with green grass, it would simply pass as one of several small hills which break the flat of the rich plain, girded in on all sides by higher mountains, which rise, in February at least, into vast snowy heights in the further distance. Still Arezzo has distinctly the character of a hill city, not of a river city; the hill counts for a good deal, while the river counts for nothing. The best points for a general view from below will be found on the town wall, a little way to the left of the railway station; while to look down on Arezzo we must climb to the castle in the eastern corner of the city, whose Medicean fortifications look strong enough without, but which, within, has gardens and fig trees level with the walls, and rabbits running about at large among them. The castle therefore forms no special object in the general view; it simply passes as a more marked part of the line of the city walls. These last remain in their whole circuit, except where they have been broken down to make the approach to the railway; surely a new gate would have been a better way of compassing this object. A town wall standing free, as those of Arezzo stand in nearly their whole range, is always a striking object, and one whose circuit it is pleasant and instructive to make. And it has a special interest in some cities, of which Arezzo is one, which have, so to speak, a show side. One side lies open to the world; the ancient roads, the modern railway, approach it; the city dies away into the country by gradually descending suburbs. On the other side, the wall suddenly parts the inhabited town, sometimes from actual desolation, at all events from open fields; the hill rises sheer above whatever lies beyond it. So it is with the north-eastern side of Arezzo, if we go behind the cathedral and the castle; we have not fully taken in the lie of the city without taking this walk to its rear. Still we must not look to the walls of Arezzo for the special interest of some other walls. They will not give us either Roman or Etruscan blocks, nor yet the picturesque outline of mediæval towers and gateways. The walls put on their present aspect in Medicean times, and over one of the gates we see an inscription which illustrates one stage of a tyrant's progress. The first avowed sovereign Cosmo appears as "Duke of Florence and Siena." He had inherited one enslaved commonwealth; he had himself enslaved another; meanwhile he was waiting for the fitting reward of such exploits in the higher rank and more sounding title of a Grand Duke of Tuscany.

In the general view of Arezzo there can be hardly said to be any one dominant object. If the castle made any show, it and the cathedral church, standing nearly on the same level on the highest ground in the town, would stand well side by side. As it is, the body of the *duomo* is the prominent feature in the view. But it is hardly a dominant feature. It is the only building whose body shows itself, but it rises among a crowd of towers, ecclesiastical and municipal, and one of them, the great campanile of St. Mary *della Pieve*, though the body of its church does not show itself far below, is a distinct rival to the cathedral, and utterly dwarfs its small and modern, though not ungraceful, octagon tower. These two churches form the two greatest architectural objects in Arezzo. The municipal element does not show itself so largely as might be looked for. The town-house is there, and the town-tower, and that hard by the *duomo*; but they do not hold, even comparatively, anything like the same position as their fellows in the great Florentine piazza. Perhaps this is not wonderful in a city which was so largely Ghibelin, and whose most noted historical character was a fighting bishop. Guy Tarlati, bishop and lord of Arezzo, keeps—though not on its old site—his splendid tomb in the *duomo*, on which are graven the names and likenesses of the castles which he won, and how King Lewis of Bavaria took the Lombard crown at his hands. But Arezzo has little or nothing to show in the way of houses or palaces or of street arcades. Its most striking building besides the churches is the front of that called the *Fraternità dei Laici*, in the open sloping space which seems to mark the forum of Arretium. This is a work in the mixed style of the fourteenth century, but so rich and graceful in its detail as to disarm criticism. Within, it contains the public library and museum. This last has much to show in many ways; most striking of all, because thoroughly local, are the huge tusks and other remains of the fossil elephants and other vast beasts of bygone days. The valley of the Chiana is full of them. Naturally enough, in the early days of science, when elephants' bones were no longer thought to be those of giants, they were set down as relics of the Gætulian beasts of Hannibal.

Something may be picked up here and there in the other churches of Arezzo; but it is *Santa Maria della Pieve* which is the real object of study. The *duomo* is absolutely without outline; it is a single body with nothing to break it, and nothing to finish it at either end. But its proportions within come somewhat nearer to Northern ideas than is common in the Italian Gothic, and its apse specially reveals the German hand to which tradition attributes the building. The church of *La Pieve* is of a higher order. It has real shape within and without. Its four arms should support a cupola, only the cupola has never been finished; the apse is in the very best form of the Italian Romanesque; the west front is called a copy of Pisa; but neither its merits nor its defects seem borrowed from that model. Part of it is sham, which nothing at Pisa is, while the small arcades stand out free, as at Lucca, but not at Pisa. The front is a wonderful display of column capitals of all kinds, from the Corinthian column used up again in its lowest range to the fantastic devices of the small ranges above them. The arch and the entablature are both used; so they are in the apse: so they are within. For the choir has a real triforium, and that triforium shows this strange falling back on the construction of the Greek. The arches below are round; those which should support the cupola, as well as those of the nave, are pointed, the latter rising from columns of prodigious height. The internal effect is like nothing else; it is quite un-Italian; it is as little like anything English or French; the arches, but not the columns, suggest the memory of Aquitaine. The south side has been rebuilt. Perhaps the work was physically needful: but it has involved the destruction of the substructure of the ancient building on the site of which the church stands. The columns in the west front seem to be the only remains of Arretium as distinguished from Arezzo. The "Tyrrhena regum progenies" have here left but small traces behind them.

CORTONA.

From Arezzo the next stage will naturally be to the hill on whose height

> ... Cortona lifts to heaven
>> Her diadem of towers.

If the journey be made on a market or fair day, the space between the walls and the station at Arezzo may be seen crowded with white oxen, suggesting the thought of triumphs and triumphal sacrifices. Their race, it was said, prayed to the gods that Marcus and Julian might not win victories which would lead to their destruction. And the prayer seems to have been answered, as the breed specially connected with Clitumnus has clearly not died out, even by the banks of Clanis. The journey is not a long one; yet, if we had time to see everything, we might well wish to break it, as we pass by the hill of Castiglione Fiorentino, with its walls and towers. That strong and stern hill-fortress comes in well between Arezzo and Cortona. Arezzo covers a hill, but it can hardly be said to stand on a hill-top; Castiglione distinctly does stand on a hill-top; Cortona sits enthroned on a height which it would hardly be straining language to speak of as a mountain. We have now come to a site of the oldest class, the stronghold on the height, like Akrokorinthos and the Larissa of Argos. But at Argos and Corinth the mountain-fortress became, at a later stage, the citadel of the younger city which grew up at the mountain's foot. But at Cortona, as at greater Perugia, the city still abides on the height; it has never come down into the plain. So it has remained at Laon; so it has become at Girgenti, where the vast lower space of the later Akragas is forsaken, and the modern town has shrunk up within the lines of the ancient acropolis. From the ground below Cortona we look up to a city like those of old, great and fenced up to heaven; the "diadem of towers" is there still, though it is now made up of a group of towers, ecclesiastical, municipal, and military, none of them of any account in itself, but each of which joins with its fellows to make up an effective whole. At Cortona indeed, as at Argos and Corinth, there is an upper and a lower city, and the upper city is pretty well forsaken. But while at Argos and Corinth the lower city stands in the plain, and the acropolis soars far above it, at Cortona the lower city itself stands so high up the hill that it is only when we reach it that we fully understand that there is a higher city still. The site itself belongs so thoroughly to the oldest days of our European world that there is a certain kind of satisfaction in finding that the main interest of the place belongs to those oldest days. We are well pleased that everything of later times is of quite a secondary character, and that the distinctive character of Cortona is to be the city of the Etruscan walls.

In truth, a certain degree of wonder is awakened by the fact that Cortona exists at all. It would have been by no means amazing if we had found only its ruins, as on so many other old-world sites for which later times have found no use. Great in its earliest days, foremost among the Etruscan cities of the mountains, Cortona has never been great in any later age. As a Roman city and colony it was of so little account that, even in Italy, where bishops are so thick upon the ground, it did not become a bishopric till the fourteenth century. Just at that time came its short period of anything like importance among the cities of mediæval Italy. Sold to Florence early in the fifteenth century, it has ever since followed the fortunes of the ruling city. Yet through all these changes Cortona has managed to live on, though we can hardly say to flourish. It still keeps the character of a city, though a small and mean one, inhabited by a race of whom the younger sort seem to have nothing to do but to run after the occasional visitor. One ragged urchin offers to accompany him to the cathedral; another persists in following him round nearly the whole circuit of the ancient walls. This last is too bad; a walk round the walls of Cortona is emphatically one of those things which are best enjoyed in one's own company.

As an Italian city which has lived, though in rather a feeble way, through the regular stages of Roman colony and mediæval commonwealth, Cortona has of course its monuments which record those periods of its being. There are some small fragments of Roman work, but nothing that can be called a Roman building. There is a crowd of churches and monasteries, but none of any great architectural value, though some contain works of importance in the history of painting. It perhaps marks the position of Cortona as a comparatively modern bishopric that its cathedral church is in no sort the crowning building of the city. The *duomo* stands about half-way up the height within the town, on a corner of the walls. Its elegant *Renaissance* interior has been already spoken of; it seems to have supplanted a Romanesque building the columns of which may have been used again. The point in the upper city where we should have looked for the *duomo* is occupied by the Church of St. Margaret, that is, Margaret of Cortona, described over her portal as "pœnitens Margarita," marked off thereby alike from the virgin of Antioch and from the matron of Scotland. The municipal buildings are not remarkable, though one wall of the Palazzo Pretorio must be a treasure-house for students of Italian heraldry, thickly coated as it is with the arms of successive *podestas*. Of private palaces the steep and narrow streets contain one or two; but it is not on its street architecture that Cortona can rest its claim to fame. From the lower city, with its labyrinth of streets, we may climb to the acropolis. Here, around the Church of St. Margaret, all seems desolate. The Franciscan convent on the slope below it lies in ruins—not an usual state for an Italian building. The castle above, fenced in by its ditch, seems as desolate as everything around, save the new or renewed fabric of St. Margaret's. This height is the point of view to which the visitor to Cortona will be first taken, if he listens to local importunity. A noble outlook it is; but the traveller can find points of view equally noble in the course of the work which should be done first of all—that of compassing the mighty wall which is the thing that makes Cortona what it is.

The process of going to the back of the city, which may be done in some measure at Arezzo, may be done in all its fulness at Cortona. Happily, very nearly the whole wall can be compassed without, and in by far the greater part of its course more or less of the old Etruscan rampart remains. In many places the mighty stones still stand to no small height, patched of course and raised with work of later times, but still standing firmly fixed as they were laid when Cortona stood in the first rank among the cities of the Rasena. Not that there is reason to attribute any amazing antiquity to these walls. We must remember that the Etruscan cities kept their local freedom till the days of Sulla, and that some Etruscan works are later than some Roman works. The masonry is by no means of the rough and early kind; yet the one remaining gate, unluckily blocked, is square-headed, and might almost have stood at Mykênê. On the highest point, the hindermost point, the wildest and most desolate point, where, though just outside an inhabited city, we feel as if we were in a land forsaken of men, the Etruscan wall has largely given way to the mediæval fortress whose present aspect dates from Medicean days. But it has given way only to leave one of the grandest pieces of the whole wall standing as an outpost in the rear of the city, overhanging the steepest point of the whole hill. The Etruscan wall, the Medicean castle, one seeming to stand as forsaken and useless as the other, form a summary of the history of Cortona in stone and brick.

From the walls we may well turn to the Museum, to see the tombs and the other relics of the men who reared them. Pre-eminent among them, the glory of the Cortonese collection, as the Chimæra is the glory of the Florentine collection, is a magnificent bronze lamp, wrought with endless mythological figures. Near it stands the painting of a female head, which we might at first take for the work of *Renaissance* hands, and in which those who are skilled in such matters profess to recognize the existing type of Cortonese beauty.

The painting however dates from the days when Cortona was still Etruscan. Perugia keeps her ancient inhabitants themselves, in the shape at least of their skulls and skeletons. At Cortona the remote mothers, it may be, of her present people live more vividly in the form of the Muse whose features were copied, it may be nineteen hundred years back, from the living countenance of one of them.

PERUGIA.

The hill-city of Perugia supplies an instructive contrast with the hill-city of Cortona. The obvious contrast in the matter of modern prosperity and importance is an essential part of the comparative history. Cortona has through all ages lived on, but not much more than lived on. Perugia has, through all ages, kept, if not a place in the first rank of Italian cities, yet at any rate a high place in the second rank. She never had the European importance of Venice, Genoa, Florence, Naples, and Milan, or of Pisa in her great days. But in the purely Italian history of all ages Perugia keeps herself before our eyes, as a city of mark, from the wars of the growing Roman commonwealth down to the struggle which in our own days freed her from a second Roman yoke. In the civil wars of the old Rome, in the wars between the Goth and the New Rome, in the long tale of the troubled greatness of mediæval Italy, Etruscan Perusia, Roman Augusta Perusia, mediæval and modern Perugia, holds no mean place. And the last act in the long drama is not the least notable. It sounds like a bit out of Plutarch's "Life of Timoleôn," when we read or when we remember how, twice within our own days, little more than twenty and thirty years back, the fortress of the tyrants was swept away, as the great symbolic act which crowned the winning back of freedom in its newest form. When a city has such a tale as this to tell, we do not expect, we do not wish, that its only or its chief interest should gather round the monuments of an early and almost præhistoric day of greatness. At Cortona we are glad that things Etruscan are undoubtedly uppermost. At Perugia we are glad that things Etruscan are there to be seen in abundance; but we also welcome the monuments of Roman days, pagan and Christian; we welcome the streets, the churches, and palaces of mediæval times, and even the works of recent times indeed. The Place of Victor Emmanuel with the modern buildings which crown it, supplanting the fortress of Pope Paul, as that supplanted the houses, churches, and palaces of earlier times, is as much a part of the history of Perugia as the Arch of Augustus or the Etruscan wall itself.

The difference between the abiding greatness of Perugia and the abiding littleness of Cortona is no doubt largely due to the physical difference of their sites. Both are hill-cities, mountain-cities, if we will; but they sit upon hills of quite different kinds. The hill of Perugia is better fitted for growth than the hill of Cortona. Cortona sits on a single hill-top. Perugia sits, not indeed on seven hills, but on a hill of complicated outline, which throws out several—possibly seven—outlying, mostly lower, spurs, with deep valleys between them. The Etruscan and Roman city took in only the central height, itself of a very irregular shape and at some points very narrow. The lower and outlying spurs were taken within the city in later times. Hence it is only in a small part of their circuit that the original walls remain the present external walls; it is only on part of its western side that we can at all go behind Perugia. But the lower city is still thoroughly a hill-city. The hill of Perugia is lower than the hill of Cortona, while the city of Perugia is vastly greater than the city of Cortona. But Perugia is as far removed as Cortona from coming down into the plain. On the little hill of Arezzo such a process could happen, and it has happened. Not so with the loftier seats of its neighbours. Cortona is not likely to grow; Perugia very likely may. But it will take a long period of downward growth before unbroken dwellings of men stretch all the way from its railway station to its municipal palace.

At Perugia, as becomes its history, no one class of monuments draws to itself exclusive, or even predominant, attention. Perhaps, on the whole, the municipal element is the most striking. The vast pile of the public palace, its grand portal, its bold ranges of windows, its worthy satellites, the Exchange, and the great fountain with its marvels of sculpture, utterly outdo, as the central points of the city, the lofty but shapeless and unfinished cathedral which stands opposite to them. And at this point, the Church and the commonwealth are the only rivals; the remains of earlier times do not come into view. For them we must seek, but at no great distance. Go down from the central height, and stand on the bridge which spans the *Via Appia* of Perugia, a strange namesake for the *Via Appia* of Rome. There the walls of the Etruscan city, rising on the one side above the houses, on the other above one of the deep valleys, form the main feature. And, if they lose in effect from the modern houses built upon them, the very incongruity has a kind of attractiveness, as binding the two ends of the story together. From this point of view, Perugia is specially Perugian. And, if the walls are less perfect than those of Cortona, they have something that Cortona has not. The Arch of Augustus, the barrier between the older and the newer city, spans the steep and narrow street fittingly known as *Via Vecchia*. At Perugia the name of Augustus suggests the thought whether he really made the bloody sacrifice to the *manes* of his uncle with which some reports charge him. The gate at least makes no answer, save that we see that the Roman built on the foundations of the Etruscan, save that the legend of "Augusta Perusia" is itself a record of destruction and revival. The gateway, tall, narrow, gloomy, the Roman arch springing from two vast Etruscan towers, is a contrast indeed to such strictly architectural designs as the two gates of Autun. The Roman builder was evidently cramped by the presence of the older work. In fact the general character of the gateway has more in common with the endless mediæval gateways and arches which span the streets of Perugia. Of really better design, though blocked and in a less favourable position, is the other gateway, the *Porta Martis*, which now makes part of the substructure of the new piazza, as it once did of that of the papal fortress. And he who looks curiously will find out, not indeed any more Roman gateways, but the jambs from which at least two other arches, either Roman or Etruscan, once sprang.

The walls and gateways of a city can hardly be called its skeleton, but they are in some sort its shell. And at Perugia the body within the shell was of no mean kind. Take away every great public building, church, or palace, and Perugia itself, its mere streets and houses, would have a great deal to show. With no grand street arcades like Bologna, few or no striking private palaces like Venice and Verona, Perugia once had streets after streets—the small and narrow streets not the least conspicuously—of a thoroughly good and simple style of street architecture. Arched doors and arched windows are all, and they are quite enough. Some are round, some are pointed; some are of brick, some of stone; and those of brick with round arches are decidedly the best. But never were buildings more mercilessly spoiled than the Perugian houses. As in England mediæval houses are spoiled to make bigger windows, so at Perugia they are spoiled to make smaller windows. Most of the doorways and windows are cut through and blocked, and an ugly square hole is bored to do the duty of the artistic feature which is destroyed. No land has more to show in the way of various forms of beauty than Italy; but when an Italian does go in for ugliness he beats all other nations in carrying out his object.

Perugia, we need hardly say, is a city of paintings, and it is as receptacles for paintings that its churches seem mainly to be looked on. But some of them deserve no small attention on other grounds. At the two ends of the city are two churches which follow naturally on the Etruscan and Roman walls and gates. At one end, the Church of St. Angelo, circular within, sixteen-sided without, forms one of the long series of round and polygonal churches which stretch from Jerusalem to Ludlow. And this, clearly a building of Christian Roman times, with its beautiful marble and granite Corinthian columns, though not one of the greatest in size, holds no mean place among them. At the other end, the Abbey of Saint Peter, amid many changes, still keeps two noble ranges of Ionic columns, the spoils doubtless of some Pagan building at its first erection in the eleventh century. Nor must the *duomo* itself be judged of by its outside. The work of a German architect, it shows a German character in the three bodies of the same height, and its pillars consequently of amazing height. But at Perugia it is not churches or palaces or earlier remains which we study, each apart from other things. Here they all unite to form a whole greater than any one class alone—Augusta Perusia itself.

THE VOLUMNIAN TOMB.

The ancient Etruscans have some points of analogy with the modern Freemasons. This last familiar and yet mysterious body seems to let the outer world know everything about itself, except what it is. We have read various books by Freemasons about Freemasonry, about its history, its constitution, its ritual. On all these points they seem to give us the fullest particulars: we have only to complain that the historical part is a little vague, and its evidence a little uncertain. We should not like rashly to decide whether Freemasonry was already ancient in the days of Solomon or whether it cannot be traced with certainty any further back than the eighteenth century. But we know the exact duties of a Tyler, and we know that at the end of a Masonic prayer we should answer, not "Amen," but "So mote it be." Still, what Freemasonry is, how a man becomes a Freemason, or what really distinguishes a Freemason from other people, are points about which the Masonic books leave us wholly in the dark. So it is with the Etruscans. We seem to know everything about them, except who they were. As far as we can know a people from their arts and monuments, there is no people whom we seem to know better. We have full and clear monumental evidence as to the people themselves, as to many points in their ways, thoughts, and belief. We know how they built, carved, and painted, and their buildings, sculptures, and paintings, tell us in many points how they lived, and what was their faith and worship. We have indeed no Etruscan books; but their language still lives, at least it abides, in endless inscriptions. But who the Etruscans were, and what their language was, remain unsolved puzzles. The ordinary scholar is half-amused, half-provoked, at long lines of alphabetic writing, of which, as far as the mere letters go, he can read a great deal, but of which, save here and there a proper name, he cannot understand a word. He knows that one ingenious man has read it all into good German and another into good Turkish. He curses every Lucumo whose image he sees for sticking like a Frenchman to his own tongue. Why could they not write up everything in three or four languages? How happy he would be if he could light on a Latin or Greek crib which would give life to the dead letter. For surely nothing in the world so truly answers the description of a dead letter, as words after words, most of which it is not hard to spell, but at the meaning of which we cannot even guess.

It is natural that in the museums of the Etruscan cities the monuments of a kind whose interest is specially local should form a chief part of the show.

At Florence, at Arezzo, at Cortona, at Perugia, the collections which each city has brought together make us familiar, if we are not so already, with much of Etruscan art and Etruscan life. Or shall we say that what they really make us familiar with is more truly Etruscan death? Our knowledge of most nations of remote times comes largely from their tombs and from the contents of their tombs, and this must specially be the case with a people who, like the Etruscans, have left no literature behind them. The last distinction makes it hardly fair to attempt any comparison between the Etruscans and nations like the Greeks or the Romans, with whose writings we are familiar. But suppose we had no Greek or Roman literature, suppose we had, as we have in the case of the Etruscans, no means of learning anything of Greek or Roman life, except from Greek and Roman monuments. The sepulchral element would be very important; but it would hardly be so distinctly dominant as it is in the Etruscan case. At all events, it would not be so distinctly forced upon the thoughts as it is in the Etruscan case. Take a Roman sarcophagus: we know it to be sepulchral, but it does not of itself proclaim its use; there often is no distinct reference to the deceased person; at all events, his whole figure is not graven on the top of the chest which contains his bones or his ashes. But in the Etruscan museums it is the sepulchral figures which draw the eye and the thoughts towards them far more than anything else, more than even the chimæra, the bronze lamp, and the painted muse. Of various sizes, of various degrees of art, they all keep one general likeness. The departed Lucumo leans on his elbow, his hand holding what the uninitiated are tempted to take for a dish symbolizing his admittance to divine banquets in the other world, but which the learned tell us is designed to catch the tears of those who mourn for him. Sometimes the *Lucumonissa*—if we may coin so mediæval a form—lies apart, sometimes along with her husband. On the whole, these Etruscan sculptures seem to bring us personally nearer to the men of a distant age and a mysterious race than is done by anything in either Greek or Roman art.

But if these works can teach us thus much when set in rows in a place where they were never meant to be set up, how much more plainly do they speak to us when we see them at home, untouched, in the place and in the state in which the first artist set them! The Volumnian tomb near Perugia is one of the sights which, when once seen, is not likely to be forgotten. The caution does not bear on Etruscan art; but it is well to walk to it from St. Peter's Abbey; going by the railway is a roundabout business, and the walk downwards commands a glorious and ever-shifting view over the plain and the mountains, with the towns of Assisi, Spello, and a third further on—can it be distant Trevi? Foligno lies down in the plain—each seated on its hill. The tomb is reached; a small collection from other places has been formed on each side of the door. This is all very well; but we doubt the wisdom of putting, as we understood had been done, some things from other places in the tomb itself. But this is not a moment at which we are inclined to find fault. We rejoice at finding that what ought to be there is so happily and wisely left in its place, and are not greatly disturbed if a few things are put inside which had better have been left outside. The stone doorway of the lintelled entrance—moved doubtless only when another member of the house was literally gathered to his fathers—stands by the side; it was too cumbrous to be kept in its old place now that the tomb stands ready to be entered by all whose tastes lead them that way. We go in; the mind goes back to ruder sepulchres at Uleybury and New Grange, of sepulchres at least as highly finished in their own way at Mykênê. But those were built, piled up of stones; here the dwelling of the dead Lucumos is hewn in the native tufa. The top is not, as we might have looked for, domical; it imitates the forms of a wooden roof. From it still hang the lamps; on its surface are carved the heads of the sun-god and of the ever-recurring Medusa. Nor is the sun-god's own presence utterly shut out from the home of the dead. It is a strange feeling when a burst of sunshine through the open door kindles the eyes of the Gorgon with a strange brilliancy, and lights up the innermost recess, almost as when the sinking rays light up the apses of Rheims and of St. Mark's. In that innermost recess, fronting us as we enter, lies on his *kistwaen*—may we transfer the barbarian name to so delicate a work of art?—the father of the household gathered around him. He is doubtless very far from being the first *Felimna*, but the first Felimna whose ashes rest here. The name of the family can be spelled out easily by those who, without boasting any special Etruscan lore, are used to the oldest Greek writing from right to left. Children and grandchildren are grouped around the patriarch; and here comes what, from a strictly historical view, is the most speaking thing in the whole tomb. The name of Avle Felimna can be easily read on a chest on the right hand. On the left hand opposite to it is another chest which has forsaken the Etruscan type. Here is no figure, no legend in mysterious characters. We have instead one of those sepulchral chests which imitate the figure of a house with doors. The legend, in every-day Latin, announces that the ashes within it are those of P. Volumnius A. F. That is, the Etruscan Avle Felimna was the father of the Roman Publius Volumnius. We are in the first century before our æra, when the old Etruscan life ended after the Social War, and when the Lucumos of Arretium and Perusia became Roman Clinii and Volumnii. To an English scholar the change comes home with a special force. He has an analogy in the change of nomenclature in his own land under Norman influences in the twelfth century. Publius Volumnius, son of Avle Felimna, is the exact parallel to Robert the son of Godwin, and a crowd of others in his days, Norman-named sons of English fathers.

We are not describing at length what may be found described at length elsewhere. But there is another point in these Etruscan sculptures which gives them a strange and special interest. This is their strangely Christian look. The genii are wonderfully like angels; but so are many Roman figures also, say those in the spandrils of the arch of Severus. But Roman art has nothing to set alongside of the Lucumo reclining on his tomb, not exactly like a strictly mediæval recumbent figure, but very like a tomb of the type not uncommon a little later, say in the time of Elizabeth and James the First. And in the sculptures on the chests, wherever, instead of familiar Greek legends, they give us living pictures of Etruscan life, we often see the sons of the Rasena clearly receiving a kind of baptism. There is no kind of ancient works which need a greater effort to believe in their antiquity. And nowhere do the sculptures look fresher—almost modern—than when seen in contrast with the walls and roof above and beside them, the sepulchre hewn in the rock, with the great stone rolled to its door.

PRÆ-FRANCISCAN ASSISI.

There is a certain satisfaction, a satisfaction which has a spice of mischief in it, in dwelling on some feature in a place which is quite different from that which makes the place famous with the world in general. So to do is sometimes needful as a protest against serious error. When so many members of Parliament showed a few years back, and when the *Times* showed only a very little time back, that they believed that the University of Oxford was founded by somebody—Alfred will do as well as anybody else—and that the city of Oxford somehow grew up around the University, it became, and it remains, a duty to historic truth to point out the importance of Oxford, geographical and therefore political and military, for some ages before the University was heard of. When the *Times* thought that Oxford was left to the scholars, because "thanes and barons" did not think it worth struggling for, the *Times* clearly did not know that schools grew up at Oxford then, just as schools have grown up at Manchester since, because Oxford was already, according to the standard of the time, a great, flourishing, and central town, and therefore fittingly chosen as a seat of councils and parliaments. Here there is real error to fight against; in other cases there is simply a kind of pleasure in pointing out that, while the received object of attraction in a place is often perfectly worthy of its fame, the place contains other, and often older, objects which are worthy of some measure of fame also. It is quite possible that some people may think that the town of Assisi grew up round the church and monastery of Saint Francis. If anyone does think so, the error is of exactly the same kind as the error of thinking that the city of Oxford grew up around the University. It is Saint Francis and his church which have made Assisi a place of world-wide fame and world-wide pilgrimage, and Saint Francis and his church are fully worthy of their fame. Yet Assisi had been a city of men for ages on ages before Saint Francis was born, and Assisi would still be a place well worthy of a visit, though Saint Francis had never been born, and though his church had therefore never been built. It is perhaps a light matter that Assisi had eminent citizens besides Saint Francis and very unlike Saint Francis, that it was the birthplace of Propertius before him and of Metastasio after him. But before Assisi, as the birthplace of the seraphic doctor, had earned a right to be itself called "seraphica civitas," before one of its later churches came to rank with the patriarchal basilicas of Rome, Assisi had, as a Roman and an early mediæval city, covered its soil with monuments of which not a few still exist and which are well worthy of study. And in one way they have a kind of connexion with Saint Francis which his own church has not. The saint never saw his own monument; it would have vexed his soul could he have known that such a monument was to be. But in his youth he saw, and doubtless mused, as on the bleak mountain of Subasio and the yellow stream of Chiaschio, so also on the campanile and apse of the cathedral church of St. Rufino and on the columns of the converted temple of the Great Twin Brethren.

Assisi is one of the hill-cities; but the hill-cities supply endless varieties among themselves. Assisi does not, like the others which we have spoken of, occupy a hill which is wholly its own; the hill on which it stands, though very distinct, is still only a spur of a huge mountain. As at Mykênê, while the akropolis is high enough, there is something far higher rising immediately above it. And the akropolis of Assisi is a mere fortress; even if it was the primitive place of shelter, it cannot have been inhabited for many ages. The *duomo* stands, very far certainly from the top of the hill, but at the top of the really inhabited city with its continuous streets, and that is no small height from the lowest line of them. Above the church are the remains of the theatre, of the amphitheatre; the distant tower beyond it, and soaring over all, the fortress of Rocco Grande with no dwelling of man near it, or for some way below it. To go behind Assisi is almost more needful than in the case of any of the other hill-cities, not only for the mediæval walls, for the slight traces which seem to mark an outer and earlier wall; but yet more for the view over the narrow valley, the bleak hills scattered with houses, the winding river at their feet, soon to become yet more winding in the plain, and the glimpse far away of Perugia on its hill. But Assisi has a spot only less wild within the city walls, the ground namely over which we climb from the inhabited streets to the fortress. So it is at Cortona; but there the presence of the church and monastery of St. Margaret makes all the difference. The general view of Assisi, as seen from below, gives us the church of Saint Francis with the great arched substructure to the left, the mountain to the right; between them is a hill with a city running along it at about half its height, sending up a forest of bell-towers, some really good in themselves, all joining in the general effect. Above all this is the hill-top, partly grassy, partly rocky, crowned by the towers of the fortress which looks down on all, except the steep of the mountain itself.

Of particular objects older than the church of Saint Francis, a restriction which of course also cuts out the church of his friend, Saint Clara, there can be no doubt that the monument of greatest interest is the temple in the forum—now *Piazza grande*—with its Corinthian columns strangely hemmed in by a house on one side and on the other by the bell-tower which was added when the temple was turned into a church. But it is surely not, as it is locally called, a temple of Minerva, but rather of Castor and Pollux. Not the least interesting part of its belongings lies below ground; for the level of the forum at Assisi has risen as though it had been at Rome or at Trier. The temple must have risen on a bold flight of steps, of which some of the upper ones still remain. In front of it, below the steps, was a great altar, with the drains for the blood of the victims, just as we see them on the Athenian akropolis. Such drains always bring to our mind those comments of Dean Stanley on this repulsive feature of pagan and ancient Jewish worship, which has passed away alike from the church, from the synagogue, and from the mosque, save only at Mecca. In front again is the dedicatory inscription with the name of the founder of the temple, and the record of the dedication-feast which he made to the magistrates and people. His name can doubtless be turned to in Mommsen's great collection; we are not sure that in the underground gloom we took it down quite correctly, and it is better not to be wrong. Anyhow the dedication is not to Minerva but to the twin heroes. A great number of inscriptions are built up in the wall of the church. As usual, there are more freedmen than sons; and among the freedmen the one best worth notice is Publius Decimius Eros Merula, physician, surgeon, and oculist, who bought his freedom for so much, his magistracy as one of the *Sexviri* for so much, who spent so much on mending the roads, and left so much behind him. Here the state of things is vividly brought home to us in which a man could buy, not only his cook and his coachman, but also his architect and his medical adviser. And we are set thinking on the one hand how great must be the physical infusion of foreign blood, Greek and barbarian, in the actual people of Italy, and on the other hand how thoroughly and speedily all such foreign elements were practically Romanized. The son of the slave-born magistrate of Assisi would look on himself, and be looked on by others, as no less good a Roman than any Fabius or Cornelius who might still linger on.

The temple above ground and its appurtenances underground are the most memorable things in Præ-Franciscan Assisi; but there are other things besides, both Roman and mediæval. The lower church of *Sta. Maria Maggiore*, close by the bishop's palace, and which is said to have been the original cathedral, is a Romanesque building of rather a German look, with masses of wall instead of columns. The thought comes into the mind that it is the *cella* of a temple with arches cut through its walls. But it hardly can be; the arrangement seems to be a local fashion; it is found also in the later and larger church of St. Peter hard by. Besides, at *Sta. Maria Maggiore* there are the clear remains of a Roman building, seemingly a house, with columns and mosaic floors, underneath the present church of St. Rufino. The later cathedral has been sadly disfigured within; but it keeps its apse of the twelfth century, its west front of the thirteenth, using up older sculptures, and it has the best bell-tower in Assisi. And below it remains the crypt of the older church of 1028, with ancient Ionic columns used up, and Corinthian capitals imitated as they might be in 1028. Just above are scanty remains of the theatre; above again are still scantier remains of the amphitheatre; but its shape is impressed on the surrounding buildings, just as the four arms of the Roman *chester* abide unchanged in many an English town where every actual house is modern. A piece of Roman wall, and a wide arch in the *Via San Paolo* leading out of the forum, complete the remains of ancient Assisi above ground. It is doubtless altogether against rule, but among so many memorials of earlier gods and earlier saints, it is quite possible, in climbing the steep and narrow streets of Assisi, to forget for a while both Saint Francis and Saint Clara.

SPELLO.

The Umbrian town which takes care to blazon over one of its many gates its full description as "Ispello Colonia Giulia, Citta Flavia Costante," is hardly of any great fame, either as ancient Hispellum or as modern Spello. It must have some visitors, drawn thither most likely by two or three pictures by famous masters which remain in one of its churches. Somebody must come to see them, or their keepers would not have learned the common, but shabby, trick of keeping them covered, in hopes of earning a *lira* by uncovering them. May we make the confession that we became aware—or, to speak more delicately, that we were reminded—of the existence of the colony at once Julian and Flavian by the description in the generally excellent German guide-book of Gsell-fels? And may we further add that, though we feel thoroughly thankful to its author for sending us to Spello at all, yet his description is not quite so orderly as is usual with him, and that, though he is perfectly accurate in his enumeration of the Roman monuments, yet his account led us to expect to find them in a more perfect state than they actually are? On the whole, except for the wonderful prospect which Spello shares with Perugia and Assisi, we should hardly send anybody to Spello except a very zealous antiquary; but a very zealous antiquary we certainly should send thither. There is no one object of first-rate importance of any date in the place; but there are the remains of a crowd of objects which have been of some importance. There is also the site; there is the general look of the place, which is akin to that of the other hill-towns, but which, as Spello is the smallest and least frequented of the group, is there less untouched and modernized in any way than even at Cortona or Assisi. We except of course the fashion of mercilessly spoiling the mediæval houses which has gone on as merrily at Spello as at Perugia and Assisi. But that is no fashion of yesterday. The general old-world air, strong in some parts of Perugia, stronger at Assisi, is strongest of all at Spello, while at Spello there seems less eagerness than at Cortona to seize the stranger and make a prey of him. The look-out is perhaps the finest of all; it takes in as prominent objects sharp-peaked mountains and ranges deep with snow, which barely come into the other views, and the long series of hill-towns is pleasantly broken by the towers and cupolas of Foligno in the plain. The mediæval walls and towers, at all events on the south-eastern side, form a line which is not easily surpassed; the walk outside Spello, though it lacks both the antiquity and the wildness of the walk outside Cortona, outdoes it in mere picturesque effect. The particular objects at Spello are perhaps a little disappointing: Spello itself, as a whole, is certainly not disappointing.

At Spello we have reached an Italian town which is not a bishop's see; even in Italy it was not likely to be so, with Assisi so close on one hand and Foligno on the other. There is therefore no *duomo*, nor is there any other church of much architectural importance. The best are two small forsaken Romanesque churches outside the walls, one on each side of the town. One of them, that of St. Claudius, forms one building of a group by which we pass on the road from Assisi to Spello, a group lying in the plain, with Spello on its height rising above them. There is a large modern villa which seems to be built on Roman foundations; by its side lies the little Romanesque church; nearly opposite is the amphitheatre of Hispellum, keeping some fragments of its walls and with its marked shape deeply impressed on the ground. Here the amphitheatre is down in the plain; at Assisi it stands in the higher part of the present city; in both it lies, according to rule, outside the original Roman enclosure. It shows the passionate love for these sports wherever the influence of Rome spread, that two amphitheatres could be needed with so small a distance between them as that which parts Assisi from Spello. More nearly opposite to the villa are other Roman fragments which are said to have been part of a theatre; but the form of the building is certainly not so clearly stamped on the ground as that of its bloodier neighbour. Indeed we are in a region of Roman remains; other fragments lie by the roadside between Assisi and Spello, and when we reach the latter town, we find that, next to its general effect, it is its Roman remains which form its chief attraction.

As we draw near from Assisi, the Julian colony of Hispellum, the Flavia Constans of a later day, is becomingly entered by a Roman gateway which bears the name of Porta Consolare. But on the road from Foligno the consular gate is reached only through a mediæval one, which bears, as we have said, all the names of the town prominently set forth for the stranger's benefit. The consular gate stands at the bottom of the hill: for Spello thoroughly occupies the whole of its hill; there is plenty of climbing to be done in its streets; but it has all to be done in continuous streets within the town walls. The consular gate has been patched in later times; but the Roman arch is perfect. It is a single simple arch, plain enough, and of no great height, a marked contrast to the lofty arch of Perugia. Another gateway on the side towards Assisi, known as *Porta Veneris*, must have been a far more elaborate design. But the whole is imperfect and broken down; one arch of the double entrance is blocked, and the other is supplanted by a later arch. Yet there is a good effect about the whole, owing to the bold polygonal towers of later date which flank the Roman gateway. Another gateway, higher up on the same side, is cut down to the mere stones of an arch hanging in the air. This is locally known as the *arco di trionfo*. Of the *arco di Augusto* within the town, said to be a triumphal arch of Macrinus, there is nothing left but a single jamb. In short the Roman remains of Hispellum, though considerable in number, are slight and fragmentary in actual extent. Yet there is a pleasure in tracing them out. Conceive them perfect, and Hispellum would come near to rival Verona, not as it was, but as it is. But, after all, there is a certain perverse turn of thought which is better pleased with tracing out what has been than with simply admiring what still is. Spello will make the end of a mid-Italian series seen after the great snow-tide to match the mid-French series seen before it. Everything cannot be seen in one journey. All roads lead to Rome; but thirty-seven days are enough to spend on any one of them. From the colony of Hispellum then we must hurry on to *aurea Roma* herself, even though we have to rush by many a town and fortress on its hill-top, by Trevi and Spoleto, and, proudest of all, by

... that grey crag where, girt with towers,

The fortress of Nequinum lowers

    O'er the pale waves of Nar.

Marry, Narni is somewhat; but Rome is more. Rome, too, at each visit, presents fresh objects, old and new. The oldest and the newest seem to have come together, when one set of placards on the wall invites the Roman people to meet on the Capitol, and when the Quæstor Bacchus—it is taking a liberty with a living man and magistrate, but we cannot help Latinizing the *Questore Bacco*—puts out another set of placards to forbid the meeting. We are inclined to turn to others among our memories, to others among our lays. We might almost look for a secession; we might almost expect to see once more

... the tents which in old time whitened the Sacred Hill.

But those who were forbidden to meet on the Capitol did not secede even to the Aventine; the secession was done within doors, in the *Sala Dante*.

VEII.

The student of what M. Ampère calls "L'Histoire Romaine à Rome" must take care not to confine his studies to Rome only. The local history of Rome—and the local history of Rome is no small part of the œcumenical history—is not fully understood unless we fully take in the history and position of the elder sites among which Rome arose. With Rome we must compare and contrast the cities of her enemies and her allies, the cities which she swept away, the cities which she made part of herself, the cities which simply withered away before her. And first on the list may well come the city which was before all others the rival of Rome, and where she did indeed sweep with the besom of destruction. A short journey from the Flaminian Gate, a journey through a country which might almost pass for a border shire of England, with the heights of Wales in the distance, brings us to a city which has utterly perished, where no permanent human dwelling-place is left within the ancient circuit. In a basin, as it were, unseen until we are close beneath or above it, hedged in by surrounding hills as by a rampart, stands all that is left of the first great rival of Rome, an inland Carthage on the soil of Etruria. There once was Veii, the first great conquest of Rome, the Italian Troy, round whose ten years' siege wonders have gathered almost as round the Achaian warfare by the Hellespont. There are no monuments of the departed life of Veii such as are left of not a few cities which have passed out of the list of living things no less utterly. Of the greatest city of southern Etruria nothing remains beyond a site which can never be wiped out but by some convulsion of nature, a few scraps to show that man once dwelled there, and tombs not a few to show that those who dwelled there belonged to a race with whom death counted for more than life.

A sight of the spot which once was Veii makes us better understand some points in early Italian history. We see why Veii was the rival of Rome, and why she was the unsuccessful rival of Rome. Above all, we understand better than anywhere else how deep must have been the hatred with which the old-established cities of Italy must have looked on the upstart settlement by the Tiber, which grew up to so strange a greatness and threatened to devour them one by one. Veii, the great border city of Etruria, was the only one among Rome's immediate neighbours which could contend with her on equal terms. Elsewhere, in her early history, Rome, as a single city, is of equal weight in peace or war with whole confederations.

The happy position of certain hills by the Tiber had enabled one lucky group of Latin settlements to coalesce into a single city as great as all the others put together. But at Veii we see the marks of what clearly was a great city, a city fully equal in extent to Rome. And when the ancient writers tell us that, in riches and splendour, in the character of its public and private buildings, Veii far surpassed Rome, it is only what we should expect from a great and ancient Etruscan city which had entered on the stage of decline when Rome was entering on the stage of youthful greatness. There was little fear of Veii overthrowing Rome; but both sides must have felt that a day would come when Rome would be very likely to overthrow Veii. Two cities so great and so near together could not go on together. Two cities, very great according to the standard of those times, considerable according even to a modern standard, cities of nations differing in blood, language, and everything else which can keep nations asunder, stood so near that the modern inquirer can drive from one to the other, spend several hours on its site, and drive back again, between an ordinary breakfast and dinner. Rivalry and bitter hatred were unavoidable. Veii must have felt all the deadly grief of being outstripped by a younger rival, while Rome must have felt that Veii was the great hindrance to any advance of her dominion on the right bank of her own river. No form of alliance, confederation, or dependence was possible; a death struggle must come sooner or later between the old Etruscan and the newer Latin city.

The site of Veii is that of a great city, a strong city, but not a city made, like Rome, for rule. We go far and wide, and we find nothing like the "great group of village communities by the Tiber." Veii is not a group, and she has no Tiber. The city stood high on the rocks, yet it can hardly be called a hill-city. A peninsular site rises above the steep and craggy banks of two small streams which make up the fateful Cremera; but the peninsula itself is nearly a table-land, a table-land surrounded by hills. The stream supplied the walls with an admirable natural fosse, and that was all. The vast space enclosed by the walls makes us naturally ask whether the city could have been laid out on so great a scale from the beginning. We may believe that, as in so many cases, the *arx*, a peninsula within a peninsula, was the original city, and that the rest was taken in afterwards. But, if so, it would seem as if it must have been taken in at a blow, as if Veii took a single leap from littleness to greatness, unlike the gradual growth of Rome or Syracuse. At all events, there is the undoubted extent of a great city, a city clearly of an earlier type than Rome, a city which may well have reached its present extent while Rome had not spread beyond the Palatine. Such a site marks a great advance on the occupation of inaccessible hill-tops; but Veii itself must have seemed an old-world city in the eyes of those who had the highway of the Tiber below their walls.

It is strange to step out the traces of a city whose position and extent are so unmistakably marked, but of which nothing is left which can be called a building, or even a ruin. The most memorable work in the circuit of Veii is a work not of building but of boring—the Ponte Sodo, hewn in the rock for the better passage of the guardian stream. Besides these, some small fragments of the Etruscan wall, the signs of a double gate, some masonry of the small Roman tower which in after times arose within the forsaken walls, are pretty well all that remains of the life of Veii. The remains of its death are more plentiful. There is the Roman *columbarium*, within the Etruscan site; there are the Etruscan tombs bored deep in all the surrounding hills. There is, above all, the famous painted tomb, shielding no such sculptures and inscriptions as those on which we gaze in the great Volumnian sepulchre, but within which one lucky eye was privileged for a moment to see the Lucumo himself, as he crumbled away at the entrance of the unaccustomed air. A scrap or two of his harness is there still; the arms are there; the strange-shaped beasts are there, in their primitive form and colouring; the guardian lions keep the door; but we have no written ænigma even to guess at. We can only feel our way to a date by marking the imperfect attempt at an arch, an earlier and ruder stage by far than the roof of Rome's *Tullianum* or its fellow at Tusculum. In the Volumnian tomb the main interest comes from the fact that it belongs to the very latest Etruscan times, to the transition from Etruscan to Roman life. In the Veientine tomb the main interest comes from the fact that it cannot be later than an early stage in Roman history, and that it may be as much earlier as we choose to think it. It is the same with all the little that is left of Veii. We know that, except the palpable remains of the Roman *municipium*, nothing can be later than B.C. 396, and that anything may be vastly earlier. In the history of Italy, the date when Rome doubled her territory by conquering a city a dozen miles from her gates passes for an early stage. The life of Rome is still before her. In Greece at the same date, the greatness of Athens, the truest greatness of Sparta, is past; the only fresh life that is to come is that of ephemeral Thebes and half-Hellenic Macedonia.

We turn from Veii, feeling how thoroughly true in its main outline, how utterly untrustworthy in its detail, is what passes for early Roman history. The legend of Veii counts for less than the legend of Troy, inasmuch as invention and combination are hardly genuine legend at all. But that Veii was and is not, that her fall was the rising point in Rome's destiny, that it was needful for the course of things which has stretched from that day to this that Veii should cease to be—all this we understand ten times the better when we turn from the living tale of Livy to the yet more living witness of the forsaken site.

FIDENÆ.

From the villa of the White Hens we looked across to the *arx* of Fidenæ as one of the main points in the view. The hill of Castel Giubeleo seems planted there by the hand of nature as a border-defence of Latium against Etruscan attacks. Yet both strong sites and other things sometimes fail to discharge the exact functions which seem to have been laid upon them by the hand of nature. The post which seems designed as the Latin bulwark against the Etruscan does, as a matter of fact, play its chief part in history in the character of an Etruscan outpost on Latin soil. Whether Fidenæ was really such an outpost in the strict sense, whether it was a remnant of the wider Etruscan dominion of the days when the Tiber was not a border-stream, or whether it was a Latin town which, from whatever cause, chose to throw itself on the Etruscan side, it is not only as the enemy of Rome, but as the ally of Veii, that Fidenæ made itself memorable. If we accept the received story, the war which brought about the ruin of Fidenæ was caused because its people slew the envoys of Rome in obedience to the hasty, perhaps misinterpreted, words of a Veientine king. The king who thus took so little heed of the law of nations of course paid his forfeit, and the Royal spoils won from Lars Tolumnius by Aulus Cornelius Cossus formed one of the most cherished relics of the early days of Rome. We may believe the details of the story or not; but the spoils at least were real, if the witness of Augustus Cæsar is to be believed.

Each of the roads which lead out of Rome—since the railway came, there is practically only one way which leads into Rome—has its own special interest, and the Salarian way is certainly not inferior to the Cassian or the Flaminian. We leave the city by that which in its material fabric is the most modern, which in its associations is perhaps the most historic, of all the gates of Rome. The Salarian gate in the wall of Aurelian may be looked at as in some sort drawing to itself the memories of the neighbouring Colline gate in the wall of Servius. He who fought before the Colline gate, he who entered by the Colline gate, could hardly fail to march over the ground where in the new system of defence the Salarian gate was to arise. The Colline gate on the high ground of the Quirinal hill was the weakest point of Rome; it was therefore specially strengthened in the Servian line of defence. It was the point by which most of the early invaders of Rome marched in or strove to march in. There the revolted troops entered to put down the tyranny of the decemvirs; there the Gauls came in after the slaughter of the Allia; to that gate Hannibal drew near, and those who did not understand Hannibal said that he hurled his spear over it. Before the Colline gate Rome had for the last time to struggle for the dominion of Italy in the fight between Sulla and Pontius Telesinus. And when the Colline gate had given way to the Salarian, it was at the new entrance to Rome that the enemy came in whose coming declared that her political dominion over the world had ceased, but that her moral dominion was stronger than ever. "At midnight the Salarian gate was silently opened, and the inhabitants were awakened by the tremendous sound of the Gothic trumpet." And if these gates were a centre of fighting, they were also, in a strange and special way, a centre of burying. Along this road, as along others, we mark the broken tombs here and there, two pre-eminently just outside the present gate; but this quarter supplies one strange contrast in the matter of burials which is not to be found elsewhere. Outside the Colline gate was the living tomb of unchaste vestals; not far beyond the Salarian we come to the Christian *cœmeterium Priscillae*. We go on; we descend the hill, the northern slope of the Quirinal, and find ourselves in the alluvial ground of Tiber and Anio. We have now come near to the meeting of the streams; Anio is spanned by a bridge which at first sight might seem to be wholly a thing of yesterday, but which in truth has lived and gone through much from the earliest times to the latest. Broken down and rebuilt over and over again, from the wars of Narses to those of Garibaldi, its main arch is indeed of the newest workmanship; but if we go down to the banks we see the smaller side arches, which must have been ancient when they were crossed by Hannibal, perhaps hardly new when they were crossed by Cossus. A few steps further, and we come to another record of change; an ancient tomb has grown into a mediæval tower; the mediæval tower now proclaims itself as an "osteria"; but we feel hardly tempted to try its powers of entertainment. We are now fairly in the low ground; the hills of Rome lie behind us; the hills beyond Tiber which skirt the Flaminian way rise to our left; the hills of Fidenæ are before us. To the right lies the ground between the Salarian and the Nomentane road where Phaon had his villa and where his master Nero came by his end. Presently the road, and its companion the railway, pass close under hills to the right and, at one point, with Tiber close by them to the left. A little further on they pass between hills on either side, a loftier and isolated height to the left, a range of lower hills, broken by more than one stream and its valley to the right. We are in the heart of forsaken Fidenæ, in the pass which divides its soaring akropolis by the river from the body of the city on the inland side.

The *arx* of Fidenæ, now the hill of Castel Giubeleo, is not, indeed, a height like that of Tusculum or that of Cortona; but it comes nearer to them than anything to be found at Veii or Rome. A bend of the river leaves a rich alluvial flat between its bank and a hill which on that side rises steeply enough. Here the men of the faithless Latin city could look out to their friends beyond the river, over the mouth of the small but famous stream of Cremera, over the hills on either side, the Fabian outpost, the future home of Livia, far away, if not to Veii itself, yet to points further off than Veii. The view from the *arx* of Fidenæ and the view from the hill of Livia complete one another. Inland we see Rome on its hills; but we must again remark that when Fidenæ was, Rome sent up no lofty towers and cupolas to mark its place against the horizon. At our feet we see the lower hills occupied by the rest of the town, surely a modern settlement compared with the original *arx*. We go over its site and round its site, we mark its tombs, its *cloaca*, the place where its gates once were. The walk in the valley by the brook between the lower hill of Fidenæ and the hill which lies between Fidenæ and Rome brings the features of the place well out. It was no small gain for Veii to have such a confederate on Latin ground as the strong post which we are compassing. We can well understand why Rome on the first opportunity swept Fidenæ utterly away, while the existence of Veii had to be endured for a generation longer.

As at Veii, so at Fidenæ, the traces of the living are gone—yet more utterly at Fidenæ than at Veii. The traces of the dead are far more plentiful, though Fidenæ has nothing to set against the painted tomb of Veii. The city, doubtless, perished after the war in which Cossus won the spoils of Tolumnius. Strabo speaks of Fidenæ as a deserted place, the possession of a single man. Yet the *potestas* of Fidenæ—perhaps its dictator—may have lingered on, as such dignitaries have lingered on in the boroughs once threatened by Sir Charles Dilke.

ANTEMNÆ.

It is one of the amiable features of the study of historical topography that its votaries are so easily pleased. Two places may have equal charms on utterly opposite grounds. The merit of one city is that it has lived on uninterruptedly from the earliest times till now. The merit of another city is that it ceased to live at all many ages back. One is precious because it contains a series of monuments of all ages. Another is equally precious because all its monuments are of one age. A third is as precious as either because it contains no monuments at all. This last kind of charm may seem paradoxical; but it will be acknowledged by every one who has given himself heartily to this kind of research. At Veii and at Fidenæ the great merit is that there is, speaking roughly, nothing to see there; in truth there is the more to see because there is nothing to see. No doubt Veii and Fidenæ untouched, as they stood under Lars Tolumnius, would be best of all; but we set that aside among the things which it is no use hoping for. And no doubt if we found the sites of Veii and Fidenæ full of Roman and mediæval monuments, we should doubtless be glad to see them; but, as they are not there, we are still more glad that they are away. But we turn from Veii and Fidenæ to a city compared with which Veii and Fidenæ might seem to have a wealth of monuments. It is, after all, an exaggeration to say that nothing is left of Veii or of Fidenæ. The sites are the main things; but there really is something to see beside the sites. But there is a city, at least the site of a city, much nearer to Rome than either of them, of which the great charm is that it does not contain a single monument of any kind or date. Here we can, even more truly than at Veii and at Fidenæ, say that the very ruins have perished; but it is just because the very ruins have perished yet more utterly than elsewhere that the spot has a strong and special attraction of its own.

We took a kind of Pisgah view of Antemnæ both from the road to the White Hens and from the road to Fidenæ. As we before said, it ought to be examined as one of the objects on this last road; only things are not always as they ought to be. We must therefore start afresh from the Flaminian gate and for the third time make our way to the Milvian bridge. This time as our course is to lead us to one of the oldest sites in Roman history, it may be well, by way of contrast, to let the bridge call up thoughts of warfare yet later than that of Constantine. It was on the Roman side of the Milvian bridge, when the bridge itself, which he had fortified, was betrayed to the Gothic enemy, that Belisarius, with another Maxentius at his side, withstood the host which Witigis had led from Narnia. Readers either of

Procopius or of Gibbon must remember how every dart was aimed at the bay horse, and how the rider of the bay horse escaped without a wound. This time we keep ourselves, with Belisarius, on the Roman side of the bridge. We are therefore not tempted to have our thoughts carried off into quite another part of the world by the statue of a famous Bohemian saint, who is said by some Bohemian scholars to be a purely imaginary being. Our present business is not with Saint John Nepomuk, not even with Belisarius or with Constantine; we have to do with times before Rome was, when Tiber still parted the free Etruscan from the free Latin. We walk along his left bank, keeping within the bounds of Latium, but with the eye tempted at every moment to look across to the opposite, the Etruscan bank. Both banks are so quiet, both are so nearly forsaken, both come so easily within an ordinary walk from our Roman quarters, that it is hard to call up the days when Tiber was the boundary stream, not merely of separate commonwealths, not merely of distinct and hostile nations, but of nations between which there was no tie of origin, language, or religion. To be sold beyond the Tiber was the most frightful of all dooms which spared life and limb. If the debtor were sold to Ardea or Tusculum, he might win his freedom and become a denizen of a city of his own speech. To sell him beyond the Tiber was like handing him over to bondage among Turks or Moors. But our path keeps us on the Latin side, in a land which, when it was inhabited at all, was inhabited by men of an intelligible speech. We peer under a rocky cliff, the riverward slope of the hill which rises just outside the Flaminian Gate of Rome. On that hill Witigis held his headquarters when Belisarius and Saint Peter between them guarded the Pincian. But, we ask, why did not some city, why did not Rome itself, arise on a site which seems so thoroughly suited for the needs of an ancient settlement? But we have to go further for what we seek; no record tells of any settlement on the Monte Parioli. We pass on by a few tombs in the hill-side, and we more distinctly make out the shape of a grassy hill parted by a wide alluvial plain from the river on the eastern side by which we approach. That is the hill of Antemnæ, a vanished city whose legendary story may be summed up in a few but instructive words. Antemnæ was older than Rome. It was one of the towns whose daughters supplied objects for that great act of what our forefathers called *Quenfang*, what sociologists called *exogamy*, which secured that the Roman State should last more than one generation. War follows; Rome prevails; Hersilia, wife of Romulus, but so strangely mother of nobody, pleads for the conquered, and Antemnæ is merged, in Rome. We may be sure that this is the genuine story, rather than others which give Antemnæ a longer life. In sober history its sole record seems to be that in Strabo's day the town had wholly passed away, and that the site was, as now, like Fidenæ, the possession of a single man.

The story in Livy is well imagined. The city whose people Romulus spares at the prayer of his wife has a specially Roman character. Parted as the hill is from the Tiber on three sides, its northern point, the point of a rather long promontory, overhangs the river at the very point of its junction with the Anio. Hence, it would seem, the descriptive name *Antemnae*, the town before the rivers. Such a site belongs to the same class as the hills of Rome. Less isolated than the Palatine or the Aventine, it is as much isolated as the Capitoline was while it still clave to the Quirinal. Such a site, with a descriptive name, can hardly belong to the earliest times; it marks the same degree of progress as the settlement of Rome itself. Cut off as it was from the oldest Rome by the whole of the high ground within and without the Roman walls, such a settlement on the river, a settlement so like Rome itself, might well be felt to be a special rival, a rival which must cease to exist as a hostile post, but whose people might well be incorporated with their more successful kinsfolk.

Of a tale placed in a time which is purely legendary, the utmost that we can say is that the legend falls in with the appearances of the site. Antemnæ has utterly perished; there is not a scrap of wall; some stones which deceive the eye at a distance prove, on coming near, to be part of the rock peeping out through the sides of the otherwise green hill. We believe that no antiquities have been found there. But the site speaks for itself. It is a manifest fortress; the gates are as plain as if their openings were spanned by arches like those of Perugia or Trier. We look out on Fidenæ and its surroundings, on the old battlefields of kings and consuls and emperors; on the bridge of Narses and Garibaldi, on the line of march which brought the Gaul, the Carthaginian, the Samnite, and the Goth to the gates, and some of them within the gates, of Rome. We can look down on nearly the whole of Roman history from the site where once stood Virgil's "turrigeræ Antemnæ." But we are yet farther from being able to tell the towers thereof than we were at Veii and Fidenæ. At Antemnæ the ruins themselves have perished.

OSTIA.

From the nearest neighbours and rivals of Rome, from the slight remains which mark the sites of Veii and Fidenæ, from the almost more instructive lack of remains which marks the site of Antemnæ, we may well pass to a spot which lies at a greater distance from Rome than any of them, but which never was Rome's rival or even neighbour, because it was from the beginning simply an outlying part of Rome itself. This is the forsaken haven of Rome at Ostia. The existence of Ostia at an early stage of the historic being of Rome is no small sign of what Rome already was, and it may well have had no small share in making Rome what she afterwards was to be. For an inland town like Rome to possess a haven of its own, existing solely as its haven, at once marked and strengthened the difference between Rome and other inland towns. For Ostia, it must be borne in mind, was the haven of Rome and nothing else. It was not a separate maritime city made into the haven of Rome by any process of conquest or confederation. Tradition makes Ostia spring into being because it was found that Rome needed a haven. And the tradition has nothing to contradict it and all likelihood to support it; the name of the place by itself might almost be accepted as proving its truth. The foundation of Ostia, too, is placed in a period which is eminently a traditional, as distinguished from a legendary, period. It is safer not to rule either that there was a personal Ancus Marcius or that there was not; but we may be pretty sure that the events assigned to his reign really happened, if we can only keep ourselves from attempting dates where there is no chronology. Tradition then calls Ancus the founder of Ostia. The really important point is that whoever founded Ostia founded it purely in the interest of Rome, and that in an age when Rome was still in the days of her early growth.

This at once marks a wide difference between Rome and other cities of that time. Even the most famous of the early seats of maritime enterprise had the port separate from the city, later than the city. Corinth herself had her two havens, apart alike from her mountain citadel and from the venerable columns at its foot. When Corinth started in life men shrank from the close neighbourhood of the sea. It marks a later stage when Corinthian enterprise planted colonies absolutely in the sea—Syracuse on her island, the elder Korkyra on her peninsula. It was not till long after Ostia had arisen that inland Athens yoked herself to the sea. But, as the site of Rome itself on the broad Tiber showed that men had even then learned to understand the value of sites widely different from Tusculum on her height or Veii with her encircling brooks, so the creation of Ostia proves yet more. Rome, far more distant from the sea than Corinth, Megara, or even Athens, had already learned that a hold on the sea was needful for her power. There could have been nothing like it in Italy. There were inland cities and there were maritime cities; but there was no inland city which had put forth a maritime outpost at such a distance. Indeed, no other city had put forth such an outpost at all, maritime or otherwise. For Ostia was not a colony, not a dependency. It had no separate being of its own. It was a limb of Rome transplanted to a distance of fifteen Italian miles from the main body.

Ostia, then, called into being because Rome stood on the Tiber, is eminently a child of the Tiber. But Father Tiber is unluckily one of those fathers who do not scruple to swallow up their own children. He has changed his course, and he has changed it in a way which is not a little dangerous for what is still left of Ostia. The diggings which have been carried on by the Italian Government are most praiseworthy, and they have brought to light much that is most interesting and instructive. But streets, storehouses, temples, theatres, will in vain be dug out if the ravenous river god is to gulp them down as soon as they are well dug out. At the present moment one street, with its pavement laid bare, with its buildings still standing on each side, leads in a perilous manner into the stream. That is to say, one end is gone; the rest will soon follow; the pieces of wall nearest to the stream are crumbling to their fall. Surely it would be well to imitate in the haven of Ancus the work done for the mother-city by his successor. Fence in the flood, as the elder Tarquin fenced it in beside the mouth of the *cloaca maxima*; make a strong wall of defence against the waters, and the remains which are left of Ostia may abide as long as the *cloaca maxima* itself.

And what is left of Ostia is indeed worth preserving. Only a small part of the town has as yet been dug out; but, even as it is, Ostia is becoming a fair rival to Pompeii. The interest, indeed, is of a somewhat different kind in the two places. Pompeii will come first with the artist and Ostia with the historian. Nothing of any moment ever happened at Pompeii except the destruction and the discovery of Pompeii itself. But a great deal happened at Ostia, and that at widely distant dates. It is perhaps needless to mention that one thing which is said to have happened at Ostia never happened either there or anywhere else—namely, destruction by the Saracens in the *fifth* century, which is recorded indeed in Murray's "Handbook," but which was certainly unknown to Procopius. Ostia, destroyed by Marius, restored by Sulla, was failing in the days of Strabo to discharge its duty as the haven of Rome. It had yielded to the same enemy which afterwards overcame Ravenna and Pisa; the silt of Father Tiber was too much for it. Yet, notwithstanding this misfortune, notwithstanding the change which it led to, when Claudius found it needful to transfer the harbour of Rome to Portus on the other side of the river, Ostia contrived to live on through all disadvantages. For it has many and great buildings later than Strabo and Claudius, among them an Imperial house with graceful columns, which contains the famous shrine of Mithras. There is abundant evidence that all through the second century of our æra great architectural works were carried on at Ostia. Besides the palace, there is the great central temple, be it of Jupiter or of Vulcan, standing so proudly on its steps. There is a theatre whose columns and inscriptions supply no small materials for study, a theatre of which it might be too much to say that it suggests those of Orange or Taormina, but which certainly suggests that of Arles.

In the sixth century Procopius describes Ostia as lacking walls, and he complains that the road from Ostia to Rome did not follow the course of the river, and was therefore useless as a towing-path. This is eminently true still. The road goes through scenery of various kinds, some rather English-looking, though none very striking; the Tiber makes a far less important feature than we might have looked for. But, if Ostia had no walls in the days of Belisarius, it had no lack of walls in earlier days. The most interesting, from one point of view, among the ruins of Ostia are the remains, forming part of two sides of a square, of the primitive wall, a dry wall of massive stones, belonging no doubt to the period of the first foundation. These were clearly ruinous when the later brick buildings were reared; the wall was broken down, and men built against and upon it; they plastered it; they chamfered its stones for the convenience of plastering, as best suited their purpose. The flourishing town of the second century may well have been wall-less. Rome herself at that date had no defence. The wall of Servius had ceased to serve any military purpose, and the wall of Aurelian was not yet.

The history of Ostia from the ninth century onwards, from the vain attempt of Gregory the Fourth to turn Ostia into *Gregoriopolis*, belongs to another, though almost adjacent, site. New Ostia, with its castle, its cathedral, its gateway, its one or two narrow streets, but with seemingly hardly a dozen inhabitants, is a sadder sight than old Ostia, with no inhabitant except the stalwart *custode*, who defends himself against Ostian air by daily doses of quinine. Yet the castle of Cardinal Estouteville ranks high among picturesque fortresses; the cathedral shows a mixture of classical and Gothic detail for which nothing in Rome prepares us; fragments of ancient work lie around; the staircase of the bishop's palace, the palace of the first among cardinals, is rich in ancient inscriptions. But we hasten on to the older site. There is something specially striking in its half-excavated state. We tread the ancient pavement, between the ancient houses, of a street dug out of a cornfield on either side. The wall of Ancus loses itself in a bank of earth. Here a house, there a temple, is dug out, leaving just space enough to see it among surrounding blades of corn. At Pompeii, too, the diggings are not finished; but there one part is dug, another is not; here we thread our way along what is dug with the far greater mass of the undug to right and left of us. So far we are content; the undug may soon be promoted to the state of the dug, and Mother Earth is a safe keeper of antiquities. It is otherwise with Father Tiber. When he is close on one side of us, there is, as our guide truly tells us, no small danger. He once, as Horace witnesses, set forth to destroy the monuments of Numa at Rome; he is clearly minded to do the like by the monuments of Numa's grandson at Ostia.

THE ALBAN MOUNT.

What is the common point of connexion between all the lands and places which bear the name of Alba, Albania, or something like it? They lie so far apart, they are inhabited by people of such utterly different nations and languages, that it is strange if there be any point of connexion among them, while it is at least as strange if the name has settled down on so many remote spots by sheer accident only. We must not forget that our own land has an interest in the question: we dwell in the Isle of Albion, and its northern part is specially Albanach or Albany. An English lady living on the eastern shore of the Hadriatic was lately complimented by a Scotch lady because, being an Albanian, she spoke such good English. It was afterwards suggested to her that she might have answered with a *tu quoque* or something more; the Englishwoman was no Albanian; the Scotchwoman in a certain sense was. But have Albanians of either of these kinds anything to do either with the Duke of Al*v*a—for in his tongue "non aliud est *vive*re quam *bib*ere"—or with the Albania beyond the Euxine? Then again it is singular to read, say in Dionysios of Halikarnassos, the local wars of Rome and Alba Longa described under exactly the same gentile names as those by which Imperial Anna describes strife between the New Rome and those Ghegs and Tosks who have again begun to make themselves famous. It is Ῥωμαῖοι and Ἀλβανοί in both cases, without the change of jot or tittle. In this case, at least, we believe that philologers would deny the slightest kindred between the names; but the casual identity is thereby only made the more startling. A malicious critic might say that Anna's Romans were as unlike old Romans as her Albanians could be unlike the men of Alba Longa. But her Romans did at least claim to be Romans, sharers in the inheritance of the wolf and the eagle; while her Albanians certainly laid no claims to any rights in the Alban sow and her thirty pigs.

Rome, undutiful daughter, swept away her mother city so thoroughly that its site has become a matter of dispute. But the name lived on in derivative forms. Alba perished, but the Alban lake and the Alban mount kept their places, to play no small part in the history of Rome. There is the lake, there is the great drain for its waters, so strangely interwoven with the tale of Veii. There is the mount, with the road by which the chariot of Marcellus went up in triumph; there are still the displaced stones of the temple which was the religious centre of the Latin name. But for the fanaticism of the last Stewart, the pillared front of the Latin Jupiter might still form the proudest of crowns for the height on which the gazer from the walls of Rome fixes his eye more commonly than on any other. And, if Alba perished, she did in a manner rise again. The neighbourhood of dead Alba became as favourite a quarter for the villas of Roman nobles as the neighbourhood of living Tusculum. There the great Pompeius had a dwelling; there, according to one version of his story, his body—or perhaps only his head—found a stately tomb, though Hadrian could make his verse by the Alexandrian Shore to say that no tomb had been found for him who had so many temples. But of all villas on Alban ground, of all *Albana*, the *Albanum* of the Emperors, with its spacious gardens, its long terraces still to be traced, of course came to be the greatest. The walled station of the Imperial guards, the fellow of the Prætorian camp at Rome, became the kernel of a new town, and Albano still exists, an episcopal city, seat of a cardinal-bishop, and it still keeps its character as a summer retreat for those who, now as of old, seek to escape the smoke and wealth and noise of lordly Rome. Albano and Alba stand in somewhat the same relation as Spalato and Salona. In both cases the new city grew out of an Imperial dwelling-place in the neighborhood of the old. But there is this wide difference between them, that Alba has utterly perished, while Salona survives in ample ruins. Alba had vanished ages and ages before Albano arose. Spalato stood ready to be a city of refuge for those who fled from Salona in her day of overthrow.

The town of Albano itself contains a good many antiquities, the most prominent among which, that which greets the eye on the entrance from Rome, is the huge tower-like pile, so cruelly stripped of its hewn stone, which, truly or falsely, passes for the tomb of Cnæus Pompeius Magnus. More striking on a close examination, though spoiled in its effect by a Papal freak of restoration, is the tomb which hovers between the names of Aruns son of Porsena and the Horatii and Curiatii. Which of the two would Sir George Lewis have looked on as the more impossible? This is the tomb which so singularly forestalled the outline of the Glastonbury kitchen—before its chimneys perished—and thereby of the Museum laboratory at Oxford. A good deal of the wall of the camp, a good deal of an amphitheatre on the hill-side, and several other fragments of the earlier Imperial time, are still to be seen. But after all Albano really exists, not for its own sake, but as a starting-point for the Alban lake and the Alban mount, and hardly less as a starting-point for

... the still glassy lake that sleeps

Beneath Aricia's trees.

Aricia has changed its site; the small modern town has flown up to the level of the *arx*, to be approached by Albano by almost the only work on which we do not grudge to see the name of Pius IX. The viaduct of that "Pontifex

Optimus Maximus"—his votaries seem never quite to distinguish between him and Jupiter—is really a work worthy of Cæsars or consuls. Below it new Aricia has left the elder city, its fragments of walls and of the Appian Way, to be sought for in the valley below, the crater, so wise men tell us, of an extinct volcano, the biggest surely even in this region where craters meet us at every step. Scraps of primæval wall, hardly to be distinguished from the rocks, prepare us for what we are to see at places further out of the ordinary track; walls of the days of Sulla join on alike to what we have seen at Rome, and to what we are to see at Cori. But, after all, the "still glassy lake" to which the grove of the "rex nemorensis" has given the name of Nemi, is the true glory of Aricia. How well we remember being puzzled years and years ago with the thrilling run of the lines—

Those trees in whose dim shadow
    The ghastly priest doth reign,
The priest who slew the slayer,
    And shall himself be slain.

In these days the fault would be held to lie with the poet for venturing on an allusion which it might need a little research to take in. In those days we thought in such cases that the fault lay with ourselves; we admired without understanding till we lighted on the explanation which enabled us to understand as well. As such a process is a wholesome one, we will leave the lines without comment; not to speak of books of reference, the story will be found, in a somewhat grotesque form, in Dr. Merivale's chapter on the reign of Caius, better known as Caligula.

The ghastly priest has gone from Nemi; but the lake is there still, and the successors of the trees. Access is courteously granted by the present owner, who, we may believe, has never slain anybody, and who, we hope, may not be slain himself. But though we may admire Nemi from close by, we do not fully understand Nemi and its place among things, till we can look upon it in company with its greater fellow of Alba. That is, we must climb the Alban mount, or a good part of its height. But we go first to the Alban lake itself; and to do so we go along its rim and slide down the side of its crater. There we find the *emissarius*, so deftly cut in the rock, and which has done its work so well for so many ages. Who made it? Camillus, or some one long before Camillus? The men who built the great *cloaca* of Rome were quite capable of cutting the hole through the rock of Alba, without any message from Delphi or any design against the walls of Veii. Whoever the borer was, he did his work far more thoroughly than Claudius ages afterwards did his for the Fucine lake, which work it has been left for the Torlonia of our own day to finish. But no one, we may suppose, wished at any time to drain the Alban lake, but only to keep it in order. How needful such a work is we do not fully grasp till we can look down from above. Then we take in the strict accuracy of the name *crater*. We see the two lakes, greater and smaller, side by side, like two basins in the strictest sense, in which, at some time which geologists may fix, but which it is enough for history to say that it was long before the oldest primæval wall, the powers of water supplanted those of fire. We take in how the larger lake, with its narrow rim, in some parts of its circuit with its low rim, liable to be swollen, but with no natural outlet for its waters, might easily come to overflow, if artificial means had not been, in some early time, taken to check it.

But when we have wound our way by the rim of the lake, by the house which the so-called Prisoner of the Vatican never chooses to visit, by the rock which still bears his name, when we have crossed the so-called fields of Hannibal—yet another crater, science tells us—when we have climbed by the triumphal way to the height of Monte Cavo, we do indeed understand the geography and history of Rome and Latium better than we did before. The eye may range over the height of Tusculum and over the battle-ground of Regillus as far as the height of Præneste; it may range hither and thither over many points which have their charm both of history and of nature. But there are two sides to which the historical eye will be attracted before all others. Such a gazer will better take in the position of Rome, as he sees it, with its seven hills shrunk out of sight, a point—rather a line—in the Latin plain, with a wall of Etruscan hills beyond it. We see how utterly different was the position of Rome from the position of the elder cities; we see how she lies in the midst, at the very meeting-place of nations; we see how needful for her it was to make the barrier behind her her own; and we understand her wars with Veii better than before. But we look down too on the Latin plain itself: we look down, we believe, on the vanished site of Rome's mother at our feet; we look out on the great flat once fringed with cities, and on the great and wide sea beyond it. Here, standing forth as an advanced post of the land, we see where

... the Witch's Fortress

O'erhangs the dark-blue seas.

And beyond Circeii and its island satellites, we look on to the more distant height, in so many ages the boundary height, best known as a height by the name of Anxur, but known as a boundary by the name of Terracina. When we think how early Rome became the mistress, not only of the height on which we stand and of the kindred heights around it, but of that long coastline and its protecting heights, we feel why Rome, so early in her history, had to enter on a career of wide-spreading policy, which could never have suggested itself to a power seated at Veii or at Præneste. Rome, on her great river, with her haven at its mouth, with her long line of sea-faring subjects or allies, felt from a very early time the friendship or enmity of the great powers of the sea to be an important matter. She had to dread Etruscan pirates and Phœnician traders; the Greek of Cumæ might perhaps do something more against her than merely shelter her tyrants. We may believe or not in the connexion between the Alban lake and the fall of Veii, but, as we look one way from beside the few stones that are left of Jove's loftiest temple, we understand how needful it was that Juno of Veii should move to Rome. We may or we may not have the camping-ground of Hannibal behind us; but as we look out seawards we believe in the first treaty with Carthage; we go on to wonder how things had turned about, when Duilius and Lutatius could break the Carthaginian power by sea, and when Hannibal could make his way into Italy by land.

CORI.

There was some reason in the remark made by Mr. Creighton in the Academy a little time back, that there must be something "irritating to the Italians of the present date in the point of view which is often adopted by English writers towards Italian history." "Their cities," he said, "which are still instinct with political and social life, are regarded as museums of curiosities, which serve to awaken picturesque reminiscences in the mind of the passing tourist." Mr. Creighton was speaking of Genoa, and at Genoa and in cities like Genoa, what he says may be perfectly true. But there are other Italian cities where the political and social life at least hides itself from the passing tourist, and where the curiosity with which he regards the city is as nothing compared with the curiosity with which the inhabitants of the city seem to regard him. The curiosity is not specially irritating; it is perhaps mixed up with a certain open craving after *soldi* which nothing short of the very highest civilization can get rid of; but it is quite distinct from the endless touting and wearying which the traveller has to undergo in places which are one degree more advanced, or which, to speak more civilly, have fallen less far back. For it is only civil to believe of cities which were once independent commonwealths, members of the League of the Thirty Cities, and, therefore, doubtless instinct with political life, that they were, at least two or three millenniums back, cleaner than they are now, and filled with inhabitants who had something more to do than their successors seem to have. But the interest which the novelty of the stranger awakens in the minds of the present inhabitants—far keener, it would seem, than the interest which the antiquity of the city awakens in his mind—really does him no harm. The modern Latins or Volscians come and look; they wonder; they follow. If the nature of the country requires that the strangers be set on asses and mules, the curiosity, as is only natural, reaches its height. The asses of the Prisci Latini or of their Volscian neighbours are undoubtedly grave and discreet beasts; even the obstinacy of the mule is a virtue when he knows the way so much better than his foreign rider. But there is something grotesque in the way of going; it is not wonderful if the sight gathers together a crowd, if the travellers find themselves the centre, not exactly of triumph, for they are not drawn in a chariot; not exactly of an ovation, for they do not walk on foot; but of a not ill-humoured procession of gazers, it may even be of admirers.

Something of this kind is likely to be the destiny, at some point at least, of those who wish to carry out the full programme of the right wing of the Latin host of Regillus:

Aricia, Cora, Norba,

Velitræ, with the might

Of Setia and of Tusculum.

Tusculum they will, perhaps, have made the object of a separate pilgrimage; Aricia belongs to the following of Jupiter and the Alban mount; "Setia's purple vineyards" it may be hard to take into the line of march; but, with a slight change of order, "Velitræ, Cora, Norba," with the later Ninfa thrown in as a substitute for neglected Setia, will form an admirable group, a day's journey, which those who have made it will perhaps, at the end of a day or two, feel sorry that they have not cut into two. Velitræ—hardly changed in the modern Velletri—has itself but little to show beyond one of the very noblest bell-towers of the second Italian period, where the pointed arch creeps in, a visitor which in Italy is better away, but which at least keeps out the vagaries of a yet later time. The lie of the town is good; it stands well on its hill, of no great elevation among its brighter neighbours. Besides the bell-tower, it has little to show in the ecclesiastical line, save only the eccentricity of having its cathedral church placed as if we were in Wales instead of in Italy, at the bottom of the city instead of at the top. One or two ancient houses and modern palaces may claim some attention, but Velletri, truly barren in Roman remains, cannot be said to be fruitful in those of mediæval times. The chief value of the town is as a starting-point—we can hardly call it centre—for Cora, Norba, and several other of its ancient fellows. The view from Velletri is beyond words. We look over the fertile plain, dying away to the right into the Pomptine marshes, and fenced in by the mighty limestone bulwark of the Volscian mountains. To the right of all the height of Anxur's temple looms in the distance; Circeii, with its following of islands, rises nearer and more plainly, almost itself like a great island, reminding the visitor from the West of England of Brean Down and the Holms in the Severn Sea. But the mountains draw the eyes towards them by something more than their bright masses, something more than a light and shade upon their sides. Several of their strong points are crowned with castles and whole towns; and one point so crowned stands out as the centre of all. We see one spur of the mountain, far lower than the heights beyond it, crowned by a little city coming some way down its sides, with a tall tower rising well from the midst when the sunlight catches it. There stands one of the chief objects for which Velletri is the starting-point; there we have to look for—

> ... the gigantic watch-towers,
>
> No work of earthly men,
>
> Whence Cora's sentinel's o'erlook
>
> The never-ending fen.

Watch-towers, perhaps, in the strictest sense, we do not see, and we shall hardly find them when we come nearer; but Cora, *Cori*, still keeps the mightiest of walls, which it was no wonder that men looked on as too mighty to be the work of such mortals—in Homer's phrase—as we now are, and looked on them as reared by no hands weaker than those of the forgers of Jove's own thunderbolts. With Cori we enter on the examination of a long series of towns, whose main feature is their primæval walls, and among these Cori has the merit of showing us the walls that are the most primæval of all. None of its fellows can show such blocks as the mysterious engineers, whose work men love to call Cyclopean, piled together in the lower town of Cori, just outside what is now the gate of Ninfa. Blocks indeed of equal size we may see elsewhere, but surely none of equal rudeness. They are heaped together as they were hewn or torn away from their place in the natural rock; huge limestone blocks of every size and shape, with the spaces between them filled up with similar stones of their own kind. But the whole range of the wall of Cori is not of this primitive sort. The curious in such matters distinguish five epochs: Cyclopean, Latin, Old Roman, Roman of Sulla's day, and—the leap is a great one—mediæval walls of the time of King Ladislaus; we hardly venture to give an Angevin king of the hither Sicily the full Slavonic shape which marks him as sprung from the other side of Hadria. The stones of the first four—we have already spoken of the first of all—are all polygonal, of distinguishing degrees of regularity of work and degrees of size. The rudest wall, as far as we saw, of all is to be found quite at the bottom; the others may be seen side by side in the great walls of the *arx* which soar high above all, and which shelter the chief ornament of Cori in quite another department.

According to the nearly invariable rule, the *arx* of Cora contained a temple, and the temple, as so often happens, has been turned into a church. But the change has been less destructive to Cori than in many other places. The house of St. Peter has been built without damaging the portico of the house of Hercules—the old Latin Hercules was hopelessly confused with the Hêraklês of Greek legend—and still keeps the columns of his portico, both on its front and its sides; keeps his entablature, his pediment, the gate-way of his *cella*, the inscription which records the work of the local *duumvirs*, Manlius and Turpilius. But what shall we say to the columns themselves? They profess to be Doric, even to be Greek Doric; but they have bases; they stand as wide apart as Etruscan tradition planted the columns of the Capitoline Jupiter; the shafts themselves, instead of being as massive as Pæstum, are slenderer than Nemea. But sin against rule as it may, the upper temple at Cori is still undoubtedly pretty, to say the least, and it is really all the more interesting because of its sin against rule. Far finer in themselves are the Corinthian columns—such as are left—of the temple of the Greek Twin Brethren lower down the hill; but we can see good Corinthian columns in a great many places; the peculiarities of the Hercules temple are special to Cori. Do they not speak of the Hellenizing mind of the great dictator who made Cora rise again after it had suffered deeply at the hands of his Marian enemies? Stern restorer of what he deemed Rome's ancient ways, but votary and favourite of Hellenic gods, the taste of Sulla might well lead him to some such forms as we see in the object, yet prominent from many points of view, that crowns the height of the citadel of Cora.

But we have not gone through the full tale of the antiquities of this strange little mountain-city. Outside the Ninfa gate, spanning at a vast height the deep gorge which on that side forms the foss of Cori, rises a bridge, of days which we call ancient, but which we are tempted to call modern so near to the Cyclopean wall. Not a few fragments of columns may be marked here and there in the streets. We light too on inscriptions. Besides the *duumvirs*—one might call them the bailiffs—of the Roman Municipium, whose names are carved on the frieze of Hercules, another commemorates two *Praitors*; surely these, with their archaic spelling, are the abiding magistrates of the Latin Commonwealth—as Cicero's Milo was dictator of Lanuvium—dependent on Rome, but not fully incorporated in her substance. Then, besides the chief temple, other Pagan buildings and objects have been turned to Christian uses. In the church where St. Peter has supplanted Hercules, an altar, if altar it be, bearing rams with horns and the Gorgon's head, has been hollowed out to make a baptismal font. The church of St. Oliva bears a dedication dating only from the sixteenth century; but it is a lovely cloister of that better kind of *Renaissance* which was in truth only a falling back on Romanesque. In the church are memorials of earlier times, classical columns used again, fitted some of them with capitals of the very rudest Romanesque, whose fellows may be found in Worcester and at Hildesheim. Altogether Cori is emphatically a place for a visit. But a word of warning must be given. Cori and Norba cannot be combined so as to see both worthily in a single day. Let the traveller either make two distinct outings from Velletri, or let him take his chance of sleeping at Cori; it may not be a worse chance than sleeping at Frosinone, where sleep may be had. Then let him rise up early in the morning and saddle his ass, or, if able-bodied, let him rather make his way on his own feet along the mountain-path to Norba.

NORBA.

We will suppose that, the mutual curiosity of natives and strangers having been fully gratified at Cori, the strangers have set out on their way, on mule-back or otherwise. The mountain-track up and down, skirting the lower heights of the Volscian range, opens noble views of the higher mountains inland, of the wide flat below, and of the sea beyond. But these views are perhaps, on the whole, better enjoyed when the traveller has found a firm foothold within "Norba's ancient wall" than while he has personal experience how

The patient ass, up flinty paths,

   Plods with his weary load.

Still worse indeed is it when the flinty paths have to be plodded down, and when the weary load needs all his theoretical philosophy to persuade him how thoroughly safe he really is, while the weakness of the flesh surrounds the descent with terrors which he knows to be unreal. At last the ancient wall rises immediately before him; the hill-side, a small height straight above the path, is climbed on his own feet, and he can presently contemplate at his ease both the wall itself and the prospect which it commands. The last part of the ass-track has become so like a lane anywhere else that we are amazed when we reach the other side of the immediate height of Norba, and find how far below lies the plain from which the almost perpendicular cliffs spring to bear up the forsaken city. For at Norba the curiosity will be almost wholly on the side of the stranger; in cannot be returned in kind, as at Cori; a lone shepherd or two may come to look at him; he cannot bring together the least approach to a triumphal procession. For within the wall all is, we cannot say desolate or forsaken, for the crops are there, full and green—"*segetes, ubi Norba fuit*"—but the ancient circuit is at least empty of all dwelling-places of man. We would fain believe that the space has stood as empty as it now does ever since the people of Norba—less wise, as the event showed, than their neighbours of Cora—embraced the cause of Marius with such desperate zeal that they slew themselves and burned their houses rather than let either themselves or their goods fall into the hands of Sulla. This inference might possibly be rash; for the ancient wall fences in at least one ruin which may be later than the days of the fortunate dictator. But it is clear that Norba, if it recovered from this great single blow, gradually dwindled away, to the profit, first of Norma by its side, which still abides, and of Ninfa, at its foot, which has perished only less utterly than Norba itself.

Cori and Norba are alike cities set on hills, and neither of them has any fear of being hid. But they are set on hills in different senses. Cori occupies the upper part of the sloping hill, and the houses spread down the slope. Norba occupies a large table-land on the edge of the mountains, and its outer wall is carried along the upper rim of a steep and lofty cliff. No dwellings could ever have spread themselves downwards on the side which looks toward the marshes and the sea. But we should hardly have said the outer wall; for the height was so carefully fortified that outlying defences were placed at various points on the side of the cliff wherever the primitive engineers deemed such defences needful. Within the circuit, again, the *arx* rose on several terraces; its highest point—crowned, we may believe, as usual, by a temple—must have formed a proud object indeed from the vast extent of land and sea which it looks down upon. No other of its ancient neighbours looks down so immediately on the great Pomptine flat as Norba does, as none looks down from so great a height. Cori rather occupies a hill thrown out in front of the mountain; Norba sits on the edge of the mountain itself, though of course at a much lower elevation than the huge masses further inland. The towers and temples of the city must have had a wonderful effect from the lands below; as it is, there is nothing to mark the place but the line of wall itself, which does not always stand out in a very marked way from the cliff. It is then perhaps in some sort well that the later Norma has taken the place of Norba. On the hill of Norba we see that Norma and Norba by no means join one another; there is a gap between them which, while we are on the mountain, might pass for a valley. But as we look from below, the winding outline of the hills puts this gap out of sight, and Norma and Norba become in appearance one whole. Norma looks like a continuation of Norba; it might pass for its still inhabited part, perhaps, as at Syracuse and Girgenti, for the elder stronghold within which the city had again shrunk up. From the points where the eye can take in ruined Ninfa at the foot of the cliff, and the further town of Sermoneta crowning a hill-top far lower than the height of Norba, the whole grouping is wonderful. The view from Norba itself takes in points with which we have become familiar since we first gazed on them from the height of the Latian Jupiter. But we see them in new groupings and new proportions; the islands, prisons for dangerous or discreditable members of the Imperial house, stand out in special prominence in front of the Circæan height—a height so nearly cut off from the mainland that it seems like the greatest of the island group. Nowhere do we better understand what men looked on as a great and strong city in days when they had not yet learned that an element of truer might lurked in what, judged by the standard of Norba, would seem a mere group of molehills by the yellow Tiber.

As the whole city lay on the top of the hill, the space taken in by the walls is necessarily greater than in those towns where the hill stands distinct, the *arx* alone crowns the top, and where the town walls are placed lower down. The nature of the construction adapts itself to the needs of the different parts of the circuit. The mass of the wall is of polygonal stones, rude, but far less rude than the rudest at Cori. Without being actually laid in regular order, they have a certain tendency to fall into courses as it were of themselves, and it is not always easy to tell how far the roughness of the stone has been from the beginning, and how far it is due to the action of the weather on stones cut perhaps somewhat less carefully than the finer stones at Cori. But the Norban builders could, when it was worth their while, do something more than this. They could, when they had to make a corner, put together squared stones cut with a good deal of exactness, and when it was convenient that a corner should be rounded off, they could do that too with equal skill. This last was done at the greatest gateway looking towards Norma. Here there is no sign of either lintel, arch, or attempt at arch, to span the opening; it would almost seem that the gate itself was simply placed across the opening with nothing over it, much as at Tusculum the gate was hung between two pieces of native rock. That the arch was not known to the first builders of Norba, but that they had reached the stage in which men began as it were to stretch forth their hands towards that great invention, is shown by a ruined building—one of the few things within the wall of Norba which can be called even a ruined building—a little way beyond the *arx*. Here we have a distinct attempt at a vault for the roof; but it is not the apparent cupola of Mykênê and New Grange, nor the apparent barrel-vault of Tusculum. The building is oblong, and the attempted arches rise on both sides, from the small ones as well as from the longer. The ruined state of the building, whatever it was, most unluckily hinders us from seeing how the four vaults, so to call them, were made to meet in the middle. It must have been a strange problem in construction. Hard by is the other building at which we have already hinted as being of later date. It has real arches and masonry, like that which at Cori is attributed to Sulla's time. But it may as well come before the overthrow of Norba in his day as after it.

From primæval and forsaken Norba we go down the hill-side, learning as we go how high Norba stands, to hardly less forsaken, though only mediæval, Ninfa. Ninfa, unlike Norba, has a few inhabitants; there is a house and a mill, if not within the fortified enclosure, at least just outside it, and, if the enclosure itself contains no actual dwelling-places of man, it contains abundance of buildings which have once been so. One can hardly fancy a greater contrast than that which strikes us between the stern primæval wall of Norba, fencing in the thick-standing corn, and the wall of Ninfa, with its towers, its varied and picturesque outline, fencing in a crowd of houses, churches, and buildings of every kind, the oldest of which could not have arisen till a thousand years after Norba became desolate. All are now forsaken, roofless, shattered, forming one of the most singular gatherings of ruins to be seen anywhere, the mummy, as it has been well called, of a dead town. Ninfa was once a place of some consequence, which played its part in local history; perhaps the most notable event suggested by its name is that here Alexander III., a Pope who had so much to do with our own history, was consecrated after his famous disputed election. But its position in the deadly flat, close by a stream, led to its ruin; the malaria was too much for it, and Ninfa ceased to be reckoned among the cities of articulate-speaking men. Some freak might restore the greatness of Norba; for there is nothing to hinder men living there if the fancy took them; they cannot live at Ninfa without greater changes than a Marius or a Sulla can work. There is something specially striking in a town, whose remains are so extensive, standing so utterly desolate. There is something Irish in the look of things at Ninfa, as indeed there is in the look of a good many of the ruined mediæval sites which often meet us in this region. It is not merely the fact of their being ruined, though there is something Irish in that; the tall, slender towers, of which there are many both at Ninfa and elsewhere, have a real likeness to many buildings in Ireland. But, though the general look of Ninfa is singularly striking, there is less to be learned from the particular buildings than might have been looked for. They are spread over several centuries, some of the houses reaching even into *Renaissance* times. The church of most pretension lies without the walls; several within them keep their apses and the paintings on them, but little more. The whole is a wilderness of ruins, strange, impressive, but hardly venerable. As the ruin of a town, the wreck of many buildings crowded close together, fallen Ninfa has little of the solemnity of our own ruined castles and abbeys. As for the elements of wonder and mystery, they dwell in this region on the hill-top, among the mighty masses of stone which the men of an unrecorded age piled together to make Norba.

SEGNI.

The visitor to Segni will find difficulties in studying the history on the spot second only to those which he finds at Norba. It is quite certain that he will find no books at Norba, save such as he may take with him, which are not likely to be many. It is possible that there may be books at Segni; there may lurk in some odd corner either a hidden scholar with his treasured library, or a bookseller of that class, sometimes to be found in old-fashioned places, who dislikes nothing so much as parting with his books. But, if such there be, they do not force themselves on the eye on one's entrance into Segni. A natural and important question is sure to present itself, and—without wings to fly at once to the libraries of Rome—there is no immediate means of answering it. Is the name of Signia—now by a very slight change *Segni*—to be found in any of the lists of the Thirty Cities of Latium? The lists are many, and the traveller is not likely to carry them all in his head. He may perhaps be able to repeat the lines in which Macaulay draws the picture of many of them; and, if so, every step that he takes among the Latin cities will make him more fully admire the fitness and force of the points and epithets picked out in each case. But at Segni the Lay of Regillus fails him; he has his quotations for Cora and Norba; he has no quotations for Signia. Still Macaulay's verses are not a full or formal list of the cities; while, if he argues that Signia lies too much in the heart of the Volscian and Hernican land to have belonged to the Latin name, he is met by the fact that "Ferentinum of the rock," yet further on, has its place in them alongside of "Gabia of the pool." He turns to his guide-book—and the guide-book of Gsell-fels, though it sometimes leaves things out, is almost always to be trusted for what it puts in; he there finds only the entry of the alleged Roman colony of the days of the Tarquins, with the remark that the existing walls seem to point to an earlier origin. And again a thought may occur to him, if not at Segni itself, yet in the later course of the journey of which Segni forms a part—Were the people of ancient Signia specially skilful in the making of mosaic pavements? There is a kind of work called *opus Signinum*, a pattern of black spots on a white ground, of which there is a good deal at Pompeii, and of which the visitor to Segni will most likely see an example a few days later at Anagni. The question is hardly so exciting as the question as to the position of Signia in the days of the Latin League. But it is one which may suggest itself, and it is one which it will be hard to answer with only the resources which are to be had at Segni itself. The visitor to Segni is thus likely to find himself a little uncomfortable as to more than one point in the history of the place where he stands. And he will feel most uncomfortable of all as to the great point of all with regard to its earliest history. Still, he may for the moment comfort himself by thinking that there are those who might be unkind enough to hint that he would still be equally uncertain if he had a hundred quotations on the tip of his tongue, or if he were in a library with thousands of volumes to turn to.

But whether Signia was ever a Thirty-city or not—we may be allowed to follow the local usage of Canterbury, which speaks of "a Six-preacher"—there is no doubt as to its geographical position; there is no doubt as to the grandeur of its remains. In starting from Velletri, with Algidus and its holm-oaks and its memories of Æquian encampments on our left hand, on the right we turn the corner of the Volscian mountains, and the railway carries us along the valley between them and their Hernican rivals. We reach the station of Segni; we mark more than one town perched on the opposite heights; we have close by us, in the low ground—reminding us of Ninfa on a smaller scale—the walls of a forsaken fortress, with a shattered tower of wonderful height and slenderness; but the walls of Signia still keep themselves hidden among the mountains. It is not from the side of Velletri, but, as we afterwards learn, from the side of Anagni, that Segni on its mountain height, and its satellite of Gavignano, perched on a smaller detached hill in front, form striking features in the landscape.

Segni belongs to the same class of hill-fortress as Norba, not the same class as Cori. It occupies, not the top of a conical hill, but a table-land, if we may apply that name to so narrow a space, on the mountain itself. The distinction is well marked by comparing it with Gavignano just below, which is one of the chief objects in the immediate view from the height of Segni. The difference is just the same as the difference between Norba and Sermoneta, though Gavignano has more the air of being an outpost of Segni than Sermoneta has of being an outpost of Norba. The hill-top which Segni crowns is long and narrow, at some points very narrow indeed, so as to give to the space within the walls nearly the shape of a figure of eight. The space within is neither wholly forsaken, as at Norba, nor all crowded with dwellings, as at Cori. The modern town has withdrawn into one quarter of the old enclosure; but it has not, as in so many other cases, withdrawn into the ancient citadel. The site of the *arx* of Signia, rising but little above the general level of the hill-top, but placed well so as to command what we may call the isthmus between the two parts of the town, forms no part of the dwelling-place of the modern Signians; but under the name of *Passegiata* it does form part of their pleasure-ground. The modern town has retreated into the other loop of the figure of eight, that which lies furthest from the traveller as he draws near from Velletri, but to which the course of the road will necessarily take him first. He may enter by a gateway of Roman date, and if he so does his eye will soon be struck by the great number of graceful fragments of mediæval work to be found within the narrow streets of Segni. The town has most likely been for ages too poor to follow the example of its richer neighbours in replacing beauty by ugliness. But he will do better to keep for a while from entering the inhabited part of the town. Let him first make the circuit of the ancient walls. And he can hardly doubt whether to turn to the right hand or to the left. The claims of the left are in this case overwhelming. Long before he has reached the town, he must have seen far away on the hill the most precious of the remains of Signia, the gateway which stands, forsaken but still untouched, beckoning him, as it were, to make his way first of all to the most instructive thing which the primæval city has to show him.

But before he can reach either the Roman or the primæval gate he will have begun to notice the character of the wall. The construction is hardly so rude as the rudest parts of the wall at Cori, but a great deal of it belongs to the same general stage of engineering progress. The huge polygonal stones are heaped together; but one might note perhaps two stages, yet often intermingled—one, where the sides *only* of the stones are cut so as to fit their neighbours; another, where the outer faces are also smoothed of what is called "rustication" in late *Renaissance* work. In the first they are not left so utterly in a state of nature as they are at Cori. Their sides have been cut to the shape which was thought best for the work of piling them together. In a later stage, also seen at Cori, the outer sides, those which stand free from the scarped wall, are also cut; but it is not always easy to say how much of the change of the surface is due to art and how much to weather. At Segni the peculiar shape of the enclosure makes it somewhat hard to follow the line of the walls without a ground-plan, and a ground-plan is not to be had at Segni merely by asking for it. But it is plain that, in many parts at least, on the whole side of the hill which lies exposed to the open valley, and on the head of the whole promontory, there was, whenever the ground allowed and required it, a double wall, one on the edge of the hill, the other at some distance down its side. The most famous of the gates of Segni, locally known as *Porta Saracenesca*, leads from the outside world into the outer enclosure, at a point well chosen for military purposes, close to the edge, and commanding the path by which the traveller will most likely make his way to it. And a mighty gate it is, and one that holds no small place in the history of the art of construction. It is one of those instances which show that their builders were still ignorant of the principle of the arch, but that they were, so to speak, in search of it. They had not yet learned how to make the top of an opening out of stones really so arranged as to stand by mutual support; but they were striving after something beyond the mere horizontal lintel resting on two vertical supports. The builders of Segni had not got so far as those of Veii or Tusculum; as they had no idea of the true principle of the arch, so they had no idea of its form; all they could do was to place two horizontal stones with sides sloping inwards immediately under the lintel. In truth, the construction is still purely that of the lintel, and nothing else; but the form chosen shows a certain vain striving after something different. As such, it is no small lesson which it teaches; and the effect of the great stones thus piled together to form the entrance is striking and solemn. It carries us back from days which on our side of the Alps we deem ancient, but when the arts of construction were as well known as they are now, to days when men were making the first rude attempts towards the greatest of constructive inventions. Attempts of this kind, simply because they are mere attempts, failures and not successes, have a more ancient look than those examples where the builders were fully satisfied with the lintel construction and attempted no other. In point of fact, whatever their relative date, they are later in idea, as showing a desire to innovate on the received form, some instances of which were at last crowned with success.

It is not easy to see how this gate came by its local name. One can understand the process of thought by which the roofing at Tusculum, which has the outward shape of the pointed arch, came to be called *arco Gotico*; it is harder to guess why the great primæval gate of Segni should be attributed to Saracens. It is far from being the only primæval gateway in the whole circuit. No less than five have been counted between the outer and inner walls, and two more in the part of the enclosure occupied by the modern town, where the two lines of wall coincide. Hard by *Porta Saracenesca* itself is a small sally-port; of the others, the larger ones, like *Porta Saracenesca* itself, stand at right angles to the wall. Some of them at least show the same strivings after the arch as their greater neighbour. The nature of the ground forbids the *arx* from reaching any great height above the rest of the city; but its place is easily marked. It contains a singular large cistern of Roman work, and close by is one of those junctions of different ages which always preach to us a living historic lesson. Here is the terrace of a temple wrought with stones of the primitive construction. On this primitive work rise the remains of the *cella* in Roman masonry, and the Roman wall of the *cella* is now carried up to form a church. Now, at least the church is of no architectural value, but it is none the less a witness to the greatest of all the changes which the hoary walls of Signia have looked upon.

Landed, then, in Christian Segni, we may, perhaps, remember that one of the greatest of the Popes was born either in the town itself or in its satellite of Gavignano. But which was the actual spot? Our one guide available at the moment seems to doubt between the two. In either case we see, if we do not tread, the place which gave birth to the third and greatest of the Innocents. We find, too, that a Papal palace of Segni was swept away by the Duke of Alva in that strange war which the Catholic King Philip waged, not, of course, against the Vicar of St. Peter, but against the temporal Sovereign of the Roman States.

We are thus, even at Segni, plunged among Papal memories; we look over the valley of the Trerus across to Anagni, and they press upon us with double force. We hasten to the spot where a lesser Pope than Innocent, but still a mighty one, died like a dog after his fox-like entrance and his lion-like reign.

Iter ad Brundisium.

I. ANAGNI.

He who goes steadily from Rome to Brindisi, seeing what comes in his way by the easiest manner of going, will not come very much oftener on the track of Horace and his friends than he to whom Brindisi is the haven for Egypt or India, and who rushes thither as fast as he can along the Italian side of the Hadriatic. The three routes will of necessity coincide at Bari. To Bari the traveller who starts from Rome must add Benevento, and he may, without much trouble, add Aricia. But the sites that lie around the Alban mount, the Alban lake, and its lesser fellow—the relics in short of so many volcanoes, wet and dry, the possible place of Alba, the more certain relics of its child Albano, the path by which the chariot of Marcellus climbed to the temple of which the last Stewart swept away what time had left—all these seem naturally to form a group and a subject by themselves. So may the objects for which Velletri supplies the best centre,—the hill, the walls, the temples of Cori, "Norba's ancient wall," with neither an inhabitant nor an habitation within it—Ninfa's more modern wall, equally without an inhabitant, but with ruined habitations, ruined churches, in abundance—all these may be connected with an *iter ad Brundisium*, but they hardly form an actual part of it. Let our traveller design to start in modern fashion by railway—we were going to say in prosaic modern fashion, only no way of going could well be more prosaic than that followed by Horace; let him study his time-tables, and he will find that he can, if so minded, visit Segni and go back to Rome in a single day; he can hardly do so by Anagni. Not that we should counsel such a way of dealing with the walks, the gates, the temple-foundations, that crown the height of Signia. It would most likely be found possible to sleep at Segni. Gsell-fels, prince of guidebook-makers, recommends the *locanda* there as "reinlich und eidlich," and the second adjective does not mean that the traveller will be in any danger of being sworn at. Still some may be more inclined to go to Segni and back again from Velletri, where there is no doubt as to living quite happily at the sign of the Cock. Anagni, Anagnia of the Hernicans, is the beginning of something new. It is the first point distinctly beyond the neighbourhood of Rome. It is not unlikely then that such a traveller as we have supposed may make Anagni his first halting-place. And at Anagni he may certainly rest for the night, though his quarters may be a comedown not only from Rome but from Velletri. But if, by any chance, he takes the earlier points in some other course; above all, if he visits Segni by any course, he will be all the more open to visit Anagni. The city of Boniface VIII., almost beckons to him to cross the valley and the stream. For it is as the city of Boniface VIII., the place where he so strangely met his end, the prisoner—not the last Pope who was fated so to be—of a French ruler, that Anagni will most likely present itself to the mind. In mediæval history Anagni is a thoroughly Papal city, and to this day it keeps a Papal impress on its buildings, a Papal impress meaning something different at Anagni from what it means at Rome. Anagni did not remain a favourite Papal dwelling-place; it therefore did not suffer at the hands of *Renaissance* Popes as Rome lived to suffer. But, even in the first glimpse of the hill-city, we may well go back to much earlier times. We may remember that first Pyrrhos, then Hannibal, halted thither, each on his vain march towards the Rome which neither was to conquer. And when we have reached Hannibal and Pyrrhos, we may go back to earlier ages. There is a point of view in which Anagnia is, before all things, the head of the confederation of the Hernicans. There is no people of ancient Italy of whom it is harder to get any distinct idea than this stout hill folk. In treading Old-Latin or Volscian ground we can, even without book, call up a few personal names, a few personal figures, of particular Volscians or Old-Latins; we cannot call up the name of a single Hernican, historical or legendary. All that we know of them is their geographical position, and the one great event in their political history; and those tell us a great deal. They must have been a people of no small account whom Spurius Cassius thought worthy to fill the third place in the great Triple League along with Rome and Latium. And this, though, as having neither one great city like Rome, nor a crowd of cities like Latium, they hardly seem to form a power on the level with their two comrades. But their geographical position gave them a special importance. Thrust in as they were between Æquians and Volscians, no alliance could be more precious than theirs to Rome and Latium. They were the most exposed member of the League, the outpost of Latium, as Latium itself was the outpost of Rome. Of all the three, the brunt of the struggle must have fallen most fiercely upon them; the hills of Anagni must have looked down on many a fierce struggle with the invading occupants of the opposite range of mountains. The walls of Anagni must have endured or yielded to many a fierce attack of their ever-threatening neighbours. As we look out from one of the heights of this region to another, we better understand the political relations of the endless little communities which thus lived on in one another's sight. The ally or the enemy was close at the door; there was not even any need to climb up an akropolis to see what was coming in the way of attack or deliverance. Rome and Veii could not see one another; between them therefore there could be long periods of simple peace, without warfare and without alliance. Rome and Tusculum could see one another; but they were not, so to speak, ostentatiously thrust into one another's sight. But look out from Segni, and your chief business is to look at

Anagni; look out from Anagni, and your chief business is to look either at Segni or at Ferentino, according to which way you are looking. If in some lights the long circuit of Segni on its mountain-top is less clearly seen, the lesser hill of Gavignano shows itself in front as its symbol or substitute. Cities standing in this relation to one another could not fail to be either bitter enemies or close allies. They must be always doing something to one another in the way either of friendship or of enmity. It was then no small stroke of policy when Spurius Cassius, of whom it has been so truly said that he was the first Roman whose greatness is really historical, won the Hernican land and its head Anagnia to the alliance of Rome and Latium. He did indeed put a bit in the mouth of the advancing Volscian.

We come then to Hernican Anagnia, Papal Anagni, to a hill-city girded in by mighty walls. The hill of Anagni is not, like the hills of Segni and Norba, an actual piece of the mountain itself; it is a hill, an isolated hill, a hill so large that, no less than at Segni and Norba, the city is wholly on the height; the walls merely fence in the hill-top. That hill-top is in some parts wonderfully narrow; in the middle of the town there is hardly more than the width of the chief street between the slopes on either side. And at its eastern end the hill rises to form a truer akropolis, with a steeper path up to it, than can be seen at Segni or Norba. Round the whole of this space, allowing for some late patchings, run the ancient walls of Anagnia, and a mighty and wonderful work they are. But who built them? We must confess that we walked round about them and, as we thought, marked well their bulwarks, in the full belief that we were studying the works of the ancient Hernicans. Let no one fancy that we did not mark the difference between the walls of Anagnia and the strange and mysterious forms which may be seen at Cori and Segni. The walls of Anagni bring us back within the ordinary range of wall-building as practised by ordinary mortals. Hernican Anagnia did not come within either Lord Macaulay's Latin or his Etruscan catalogue; but, had it done so, there would have been no temptation to speak of its bulwarks as "no work of earthly men," or as—

Reared by the hands of giants

   For godlike kings of old.

The walls of Anagni are wonderful only as the great works of Rome are wonderful. They are built by men to whom it was more natural to put together rectangular stones with some kind of regularity than it was to pile together huge polygons anyhow. They were built by men who thoroughly understood the principle of the arch, and knew how to use it with all boldness. They remain, in various degrees of preservation, round the greater part of the circuit of the town. In some parts they are broken down altogether; in some they are supplanted, in others merely patched, by walls of later date; in short, they have gone through all the casualties which a wall is likely to go through in the course of two millenniums or so; but the wall of modern Anagni, as a whole, is still the old wall of Anagnia. The construction differs a good deal in different parts as to the size of the stones and as to their nature, and as to the degree of rudeness or finish in the work. In some parts the wall stands single; in others it is strengthened by further defences, buttresses rather than towers—defences, by-the-way, which must be carefully distinguished from the additions of later times. But one general character reigns throughout. The stones, greater and smaller, smoother and rougher, are always rectangular, and always laid with some measure of regularity. In some cases ranges of larger and smaller stones alternate; in one part of the wall stones of two natures and colours almost alternate. The chief material is a light-coloured stone exactly like the *puff-stone* of Gloucestershire, the material of Berkeley Castle and of not a few other buildings in that neighbourhood. This is eked out here and there by the dark volcanic *peperino*, which, towards the south-eastern part of the wall, is used much more freely. The general effect, wherever the wall is at all perfect, is stately and striking in the extreme, both in form and colour.

Now was it only a dream when we tracked out these walls, and took a certain pleasure in speaking of them as Hernican walls? We come back to our library; we take down the *Dictionary of Geography*; we turn to the article "Anagnia," and we find that by far the best contributor to the series, Mr. E. H. Bunbury, has another tale to tell. Our feelings are damped when he says, "The only remains extant there are of Roman date and of little interest." As to the "little interest," we venture to have our own opinion in any case; we should hold that so great an extent of ancient wall still bounding an inhabited town was an object of high interest, even if it could be shown to belong to the latest days which could come under the definition of "Roman date." But what is Roman date? Mr. Bunbury sends us to the correspondence of the Emperor Marcus with Cornelius Fronto. We hope he does not ask us to believe that the walls are later than the days of the philosophic Emperor. For, if he will allow them to be as old as that, we can call the Emperor himself to witness that they must be a good deal older. For Marcus himself read an inscription over one of the gates, "*Flamen sume samentum.*" He did not know what "*samentum*" meant, and we cannot find the word in our Latin dictionary. But a native explained to him its meaning in the Hernican language; it meant the skin of the victim which the *flamen* put on his head when he entered the town. We do not want to be unreasonable in our dates, if only we can let in our Hernicans at some corner. When we looked at the walls, we saw at once that they had no fellowship with the primæval works at Cori and at Segni; they did seem to us to have fellowship with the works of the Tarquins at Rome. We shall be quite happy if Mr. Bunbury will allow us to put the walls as early as the year B.C. 307. The next year Anagnia sank from a Hernican city, a free ally of Rome, into a town whose people were burthened with Roman citizenship without the Roman franchise. If we may carry back walls over whose gates Hernican inscriptions could be read between four and five hundred years later, to a date as nearly as that, we shall have done all that we could wish. They will be walls of the days of Hernican independence, walls on which Hannibal and Pyrrhos have looked.

One thing is plain, that the builders of the walls of Anagnia, like the builders of the *cloaca* at Rome, but most unlike the elder builders of Cora and Signia, knew as well as any men how to turn arches. On the highest point of the town, by the modern gate which looks out towards Ferentino, within the circuit of the ancient *arx*, we may still see, blocked, partly hidden by the modern gate, disguised by the arrangements of the mediæval castle, the double gate of the ancient wall. It is perfectly plain, but with arches thoroughly well turned, with a double range of voussoirs. A smaller arch of the same workmanship beside them looks almost as if it had been blocked from the beginning. The *arx* itself, it should be remembered, had its separate wall within that of the city, a noble fragment of which, of exactly the same character as the town wall, is still to be seen in a narrow street a little lower down.

When we actually reach Anagni, there can be no doubt that the character in which it chiefly strikes us is that of the city of the Hernican walls, if Hernican walls we may call them. But historically Anagni is so far more famous as the city of mediæval Popes that it is fitting that it should have something to show in that character also. The town is rich in mediæval fragments. The main street, in its winding courses, displays long ranges of blocked arcades, round and pointed, which, when open, must have given it, narrow and often dim as it is, no small measure of stateliness. Not a few buildings stand out with arches of vast height and boldness, suggesting, as it is fit that one papal city should suggest to another, the mighty works of Rome's absent Bishops at Avignon. Not remarkable for height, but most remarkable for their span, are the exceedingly bold arches which support the communal palace, once, it is said, the dwelling of the Popes, a building which, on its northern side, shows a range of windows which savour of France or England rather than of Italy. The houses with their staircases often present highly picturesque shapes, which in one house in the main street, where the outside staircase is sheltered by two arches resting on a graceful column, grow into a form of genuine beauty. And an elegant form of double window, two round arches divided by a slender shaft, is characteristic of the architecture of Anagni. It is needless to add that at

Anagni, as everywhere else in Italy, most of these relics of the skill of former times have been mercilessly disfigured and mutilated.

In the ecclesiastical line the other churches supply a few good fragments of the same character as those in the domestic building; but the cathedral church within the *arx* is the only one which has the least claim to be looked on as a striking whole. It stands boldly on the edge of the hill with its east end—that is, what would be east according to northern rules, for it is in truth nearly west—rising up nobly with its three apses in good Romanesque style, while a stately bell-tower of the more massive sort, though sadly marred on two sides, stands near the east end which should be west. The crypt is in a somewhat ruder form of the same style. The whole outside of the church is worth study; the inside is of an early and massive type of the Italian Gothic, always, unless in the case of some unusual merit, less satisfactory than Italian Romanesque. The sacristy contains the vestments of Innocent III. and Boniface VIII., and a good many other curious objects. The church is just now suffering restoration; let us hope that nothing very dreadful will happen to it. There, at least, seems no disposition to pull down the apse, after the pattern of the church which Popes and Emperors alike have decreed to be the mother-church of Rome and of the world.

II. FERENTINO.

Italy contains two places bearing the name of Ferentinum or Ferentino, as England contains two places—perhaps more—bearing the several names of Leeds, Stafford, Birmingham, Hereford, Cambridge, Washington, Rochester, and others more obvious. And as the Northumbrian Rochester is also very conveniently written *Rutchester*, so the Etruscan Ferentinum is also conveniently written *Ferentia*. On an *iter ad Brundisium* we cannot possibly have anything to do with Etruscan Ferentia; our business lies with that Ferentinum which, according to the Itineraries, was to be found on the *Via Latina* between Anagnia and Frusino, and which is to be found there still. But if the name of the southern Ferentinum is more certain than that of its fellow, its ancient nationality is less certain. Its historical position is Hernican; it lies between Hernican Anagnia and Hernican Frusino; yet it is also spoken of as Volscian, as it may well have become in the endless warfare of those ever-shifting nations. Yet it is in other company that we should be best pleased to find it. Our earliest remembrance of the name places "Ferentinum of the rock" among the Thirty Cities, and gives it no mean place among them. We go to the spot with the lines ringing in our ears which place its warriors under the rule of proud Tarquin himself, on the spot where—

... in the centre thickest

   Were ranged the shields of foes,

And from the centre loudest

   The cry of battle rose.

Yet, even without book, we may have been a little surprised both to find a Thirty-city so far in the heart of the Volscian and Hernican hills, and to find its warriors marshalled along with such distant comrades as Tibur and Pedum and "Gabii of the pool." And, when we come back to our books, a horrible thought presses itself upon us more and more, a thought that Ferentinum may have no right to any place in that list at all. The name seems to be Lord Macaulay's guess—among a hundred other guesses—at the manifestly corrupt name which comes next before Gabii in Dionysios' list of the Latin cities. Some read as near to our mark as *Fortinei*; so we may hope for the best; but remembering where Ferentinum stands, very far from Gabii, we confess that our hopes are small.

In obedience to the Itinerary, it is from Anagni that we make our way to Ferentino. And as we go from Anagni to Ferentino, we better take in the special position of Anagni on the top of its isolated hill. Till we have gone some little distance, we are hardly conscious that Anagni is there at all; gradually the bell-tower rises into view, and the rest of the city follows. A few miles only lead us from the hill of Anagni to the hill of Ferentino. At the first glance it may be that the spot which we have reached does not specially strike as "Ferentinum of the rock." It does not seem to stand on such steep cliffs as many other hill-fortresses, Norba pre-eminently among them. But, when we begin to follow the line of the walls, we find out that, whether Lord Macaulay is right or wrong in speaking of Ferentinum at all, he has at least chosen his epithet wisely. Ferentinum is Ferentinum of the rock. Large parts of the wall stand directly on vast masses of rock, and sometimes rock and wall almost lose themselves in one another. And the walls of Ferentino certainly yield in interest to none of our series. They are still standing through the greater part of their ancient circuit, and for the most part they are of two manifest dates, differing in material and construction. There is an original lower part of the wall, built of huge blocks of lias which we may describe as rude, but less rude than the rudest work at Cori. The height to which this earliest construction of all reaches differs in different parts, but it has in most parts been patched and raised, not only by later repairs of all manner of dates, but long before then by a construction of very respectable antiquity, which would seem venerable if it were not for the elder and more massive stones beneath it. The later work has a general likeness to the walls of Anagnia both in construction and material, and it is distinguished from the more primitive work by the same mark. The pilers of the elder stones had no notion of the arch; the builders of the later wall were perfectly familiar with it. The only complete opening of the earlier work is a small postern with merely inclined sides; but in one of the ancient gates, not far from the modern gate by which the visitor is most likely to enter, stones of the earlier date support an arch of the second date. This ancient entrance is, as usual, warily placed; the giants, or whoever they were, from the days of Tiryns onwards, knew perfectly well how to take a military advantage of any enemy who might attack their strongholds. Another gate, now known as *Porta Maggiore*, is a much more elaborate work, with its inner and outer arch still remaining. Here the gate is placed with great skill, advanced in front at a point where the wall turns at an angle. The wall may be followed, and followed to great advantage, through the more part of its circuit. One hardly knows whether to count it gain or loss that the path becomes most difficult just at the point where, through large later repairs, the wall becomes least interesting. When we have to scramble—all at least save Alpine climbers—with constant thoughts for the safety of our legs and feet, we are less able to take in the differences in the various forms of construction, or to consider the dates to which we may be inclined to refer each. In the more instructive parts of the walls of Ferentino no such necessity is laid upon us; they may be studied with perfect ease, and the outlook from the various points of their circuit may be enjoyed at the same time. And at one point, not far from the *Porta Maggiore*, it will be well to go down the hill a little way to study the long inscription cut in the rock in honour of a local worthy and magistrate, Aulus Quinctilius by name, who seems to have played much the same part at Ferentinum in pagan days which Sir William Harpur played ages later at Bedford. He founded everything that, according to the notions of his day, could be founded. Among other things he ordained that thirty bushels of nuts should be yearly given to be scrambled for by the boys of Ferentinum, without distinction of bond or free. Now is the will of this pious founder carried out? Are there any Italian Charity Commissioners to look into these matters, and to see that the boys get their nuts? Or, if the scrambling for nuts be deemed a nuisance—yet many well-remembered scraps of Latin plead on its behalf—will they devise a scheme for the better employment of the funds? Or has the benefaction of the benevolent Quinctilius, like some benefactions nearer home, been lost altogether? Two or three years ago the *Times* was filled with letters complaining how a charitable foundation in Somerset had vanished altogether, and how the founder's monument, once standing in the church, had been buried under a neighbouring barn. In one point at least the benevolent Aulus of Ferentinum has been more lucky. When Ferentinum had *quatuorviri*, they did not bury people in their temples, still less did they set up monuments in their temples to people who were not buried in them. So the monument which commemorates the bounty of Aulus Quinctilius stands in the open air clear enough to be seen, well fenced in withal, which the visitor may perhaps regret, as a little time may be wasted in searching for the key. But do his benefactions go on? We will not hint at their having been alienated by Goths or Vandals, by East-Roman exarchs or Lombard princes. Can we trust the really dangerous characters in these parts of the world, Popes, Popes' nephews, Roman princes, and Roman cardinals, who pull down buildings and steal their columns to make their own palaces and villas? Perhaps some of them may have swallowed up the funds which should go in nuts to the boys of Ferentinum.

We have been writing as we dreamed on the spot. As at Anagni, we wish—we must confess the weakness—to see independent Hernicans wherever we can. It gives us therefore a little shock when we come back and turn to our books, and find the walls of Hernican Ferentinum spoken of, without any special emotion, as "Roman." We look up again in a moment, and ask,

What is Roman? At Ferentinum the word certainly means something quite different from what it commonly means in Britain and Northern Gaul. There we are happy if we light on anything earlier than the third century A.D. Here no one asks us to accept any date later than Sulla; some will allow us to go as far back as the middle of the second century B.C. We are allowed to think that the walls of Ferentinum were in being when old Carthage and old Corinth were still standing. But we have not yet got to our great piece of evidence. Ferentino contains inscriptions much older and more important—though about the comparative importance some might raise a doubt—than Aulus Quinctilius and his nuts. But we must get to them by the proper road; we must get into what once was the *arx*, what is now the ecclesiastical quarter. Now, at places like Ferentino, ecclesiastical and domestic buildings seem like something kindly thrown into the bargain. We go to look at walls, not at churches or houses; so we get something more than we asked for when we find that Ferentino contains many houses which are worth at least a glance, and several churches which are worth much more than a glance. Indeed at Ferentino the study of walls and that of churches cannot be kept asunder. That some of the great stones have been taken to build the small and now disused church of Saint Lawrence is a slight matter. The most striking feature of Ferentino in any distant view consists of the mass of buildings which is formed by piling the cathedral church, the bell-tower, and the Bishop's palace, on the walls of the *arx*, as a mighty sub-structure. The walls of the *arx* show the same two dates as the walls of the tower. In one part we have only the vast rude stones of the first period; at another part they support the upper range of the second. The first no one will refuse to our Hernicans, to Hernicans older than Spurius Cassius; but how about the second, the "Roman" date? This is claimed in several inscriptions as the work of the censors Aulus Hirtius and Marcus Lollius—censors, that is, not of Rome but of Ferentinum. The inscription may be seen in the first volume of the great *Corpus Inscriptionum Latinarum*, p. 238, and its closer likeness is given at fol. lxvii., lxviii. of the *Priscae Latinitatis Monumenta Epigraphica*. Now Aulus Hirtius and Marcus Lollius are names of a frightfully modern sound, suggesting well-known persons of the days of Divus Julius and Divus Augustus. But no one asks us to think of them here, though we may likely enough have got hold of the Hernican forefathers of those better-known Romans. They had no such need to change their names and the alphabet in which they are written, as when the son of the Etruscan Avle Felimne became the Roman Publius Volumnius. Now our Hirtius and Lollius claim to have built what they built from the foundation; but they must at the outside only mean that they built the later work on the top of the primæval wall. And to a zealous eye even the work of Hirtius and Lollius has an archaic look about it. There are no columns against the wall, as in the

Tabularium of Catulus at Rome; the work is finished with a row of triglyphs, not unlike those on the tomb of "Cornelius Lucius Scipio Gnaivod patre prognatus." But we need not go back quite so far as his day. The further back we can go the better, but any time before Sulla will do. The history of Ferentinum allows us to carry our Hernicans of Ferentinum, like our Etruscans of Perusia, down to the Social War. Ferentinum, it must be remembered, was one of those Hernican towns which were true to Rome when Anagnia fought against her. What follows is most instructive. The men of Ferentinum, steady allies of Rome, refused the proffered reward of Roman citizenship, and chose rather to remain a distinct, even if a dependent, community. That is to say, the old Hernican city went on, as long doubtless as to the days of the Social War, a self-ordering commonwealth, with its own laws and magistrates—Aulus Hirtius and Marcus Lollius among them—subject only to the demands of military service which were needed in the wars of Rome, and sometimes perhaps to the unlawful excesses of powerful Romans.

This last fact comes out in a strange story told by Aulus Gellius (x. 3). It is an extract from a speech of Gaius Gracchus, setting forth the wrongs of the Italian allies. The wife of a Roman prætor suddenly wished the public baths of Ferentinum to be cleared and made ready for herself. The thing was not done so fast as the great lady wished; so her husband bade the two quæstors of the town to be seized; one was scourged, the other threw himself over the wall. This tale, told in the words of Gracchus, proves a good deal as to the arbitrary way in which Roman magistrates are not ashamed to deal with the dependent cities even of Italy, whatever might be their formal relation to Rome.

It is of less importance that Gellius casually speaks of the town as a *municipium*, while Livy also casually implies its possession of the Latin franchise. Such *obiter dicta* do not go for very much. Scholars sometimes get astray in these times from forgetting that, not only casual sayings, but even formal documents, may sometimes err. Thus not long ago we saw a solemn paper in which a public officer, bound to accuracy, a clerk of the peace, had to describe several towns in the West of England. We here read of "the county of the city of Bristol," the "borough of Gloucester," the "borough of Bath," and the "borough of Taunton." An inquirer some ages hence might be misled into forgetting that Bath is a "city" and Gloucester even a "county of a city." May we not sometimes get wrong about *municipia* and Latin colonies from the same kind of cause? Ferentinum was not, in the strict sense, a *municipium*, but an allied Hernican commonwealth. In the like sort, we once saw an official document from a high sheriff calling on the electors of a county to elect, not a "knight of the shire," as they had done for six hundred years, but a hitherto unheard-of being called a "member of

Parliament." Is it not possible then that Livy, and even Cicero, may sometimes use a wrong phrase in talking of tribes, *curiae*, and centuries, in ages long before their own day?

The walls then, though called "Roman" in a vague sense—that is, it would seem, simply not primæval, like those of Cori and Segni—are doubtless Hernican in the sense of being built while Ferentinum was still a separate Hernican community. The walls that we see are most likely the walls over which the unlucky quæstor threw himself. The walls of the *arx*, where we read the legend of Hirtius and Lollius, connect the Hernican town with later times. Just at the point where the inscription is they are carried up to form the Bishop's palace, and from the middle of one side rises the bell-tower of the cathedral—a very good example of the usual Romanesque type of such buildings. The church of Ferentino is small and unpretending, and a good deal damaged within, but it still keeps its main features, not only its bell-tower, but its west front, its apses, its ranges of windows. A little restoration, in the true sense of the word, would soon make it into as good a specimen of its own class as could be needed. But, unless we altogether misunderstood the words of one of its own clergy, antiquity and simplicity are not esteemed at Ferentino. The little minster is convicted of the crime of being old, a charge which, except by comparison with the walls beneath it, cannot be denied. Only, if the church be an offender on this score, how fearful must be the crime of the walls? Unless we misunderstood in the most amazing way what we heard with our own ears, the church of Ferentino, convicted of the crime of old age, is sentenced to destruction. A new church is actually begun; when it is finished the old one is to go. Happily the new one as yet stands still for want of funds; let us hope that funds may refuse to drop in till a wiser Bishop and Chapter shall rule at Ferentino.

The church at Ferentino is dedicated to Saint Ambrose, who may be seen there in the worldly garb of the unbaptized prefect, before the infant voice greeted him as Bishop of Milan. And in the inner buildings of the *arx*— buildings most worthy of a visit on their own account—strange tales lurk of the sufferings of the saint, which seem to find no place either in history or in received legend. Among other things he was thrown into a boiling caldron. Down below is another church *Santa Maria Maggiore*, some centuries younger than the cathedral, and a very pretty example of its style; which, as far as we know, no one designs to destroy. Singularly graceful, but singularly un-Italian, it strikes by the power of contrast, as it rises above the walls, or as we go up to it from the gate which shares its surname. A few other ecclesiastical and domestic scraps may also be picked up in the city of the rock. The primitive remains are the great object in all these places; but it is always a gain when the walls shelter something which has an interest of another kind. The walls of the stout-hearted people who chose rather to be citizens of Ferentinum than citizens of Rome lose nothing by having been turned to an unlooked-for use as the holy places of their successors, perhaps descendants, of another age and another creed.

III. ALATRI.

The tale of those Hernican cities, fenced in with primæval walls, among which we have been lately sojourning, is worthily brought to an end at Alatri. Among its immediate Hernican fellows that town must certainly claim the highest place; it might on some grounds claim the highest place, even if we throw in Old-Latin and Volscian rivals. Yet it is the one which has the least history. There is very little to say about it, except that Alatrium, like Ferentinum, was faithful to Rome, but preferred to keep its separate Hernican being rather than accept the proffered reward of Roman citizenship. It therefore doubtless remained a distinct commonwealth down to the Social War. And here at least there can be no question about dates. Alatri is not especially rich in mediæval antiquities; it has still less claim to be called rich in Roman antiquities. Nor does it supply us with the work of more or less Romanized Hernicans, like the censors of Ferentinum. At Alatri nearly everything that we care about is strictly primæval. We cannot reasonably doubt that both the circuits of wall at which we now look were there in the days of Spurius Cassius, and were by no means new then.

Alatri seems to have been somewhat of an out-of-the-way place in all ages. Not lying on any of the great roads of Italy, it has no place in the Itineraries, and now it lies much further than Anagni or Ferentino—nay, even than Cori and Norba, from common tracks of going and from the common haunts of men. Yet it cannot be looked on as seriously inaccessible; it may at least be reached without calling in the help of asses and mules. The party whose track we are now following—a party, be it noticed, numbering two ladies among them—reached Alatri in a carriage from Frosinone, having slept there after seeing Ferentino. The old Hernican town of Frusino had scant justice done to it by our wayfarers; as no man or book had pointed it out as a seat of primitive walls, it was treated merely as a resting-place between the wonders of Ferentino and the wonders of Alatri. Frosinone was slept in, but was not examined; yet a glance from its railway station, the point which connects Alatri with the modern world, shows that it at least possesses a by no means contemptible bell-tower. From Frosinone then our travellers made their way to Alatri, and, as Alatri gradually rose before them, they were for a while puzzled, perhaps for a while even disappointed, with what they saw. But it was not for lack of a striking object to crown the Alatrian hill-top. Of all the walls of our series, the inner range of the walls of Alatri, the walls which fence in the *arx*, are the most prominent in a distant view. Even the circuit of empty Norba, beyond our immediate range, hardly outdoes these defences of a still inhabited town. At Alatri indeed the primæval walls are so prominent that in the distant view no one would suspect them of being primæval walls at all. They are still so nearly perfect that they can and do discharge what may be looked on as a survival of their original function. They still fence in the innermost and loftiest quarter of the town, where, as in so many other cases, the ancient citadel has become the episcopal precinct. But at Alatri the episcopal precinct puts on a distinct and central character which is rarely found in Italian cities. The *arx* is not in a corner, but in the middle; the lower town, fenced in by the wall of its own outer circuit, lies around it on every side. The *arx* forms an open, lofty, and airy platform, looking forth from every point of the compass on the mountains which keep watch around—on the little towns, Veroli among them, perched here and there on their heights—on the houses and churches of Alatri, covering the slope of the hill which the *arx* crowns. It is seldom that we find in an Italian town a church or any other building standing in this way free on a commanding site, not hemmed in on any side by parasitical buildings. These hill-towns are perhaps better off in this respect than most others; at Anagni, at Ferentino, the cathedral churches stand grandly on their heights, comparatively free from all buildings except their own proper companions. But there is not the wide, open space around them which surrounds the church of Alatri. One cannot help wishing that some more worthy building, either the primæval temple itself or some more fitting successor, occupied so noble a site, a site in truth which needs—let us say either the Parthenôn of Athens or the Parthenôn of Lincoln to do it justice. But the only thing that can be said for the cathedral church of Alatri is that the lower part of its wall is part of the *cella* of the primæval temple. Here we have something even more than can be seen at Segni. We know not what may have been added in the way of a pillared front; but it is plain that, as far as the main walls are concerned, the building which was transformed into a Christian church was actually the house of pagan worship itself. And it was a house going back, not to dated Emperors or consuls, but to the unrecorded age which reared these cities great and fenced up to heaven. There is the terrace, there is the wall of the *cella*, wrought of the same wonderful masonry as the walls of the surrounding *arx*, as the walls of the yet again surrounding city. It is strange indeed to see the ordinary rites of Christian worship, the ordinary accompaniments of a Christian church, dwelling, as at Rome and Syracuse, within the temples of a creed, fallen indeed but perfectly familiar. But here we see them within walls reared in honour of we know not what—gods of unchronicled days, gods alongside of whom Jupiter of the Capitol may have seemed as strange and foreign as Mithras and Serapis now seem alongside of Jupiter of the Capitol.

Where the præhistoric temple has thus become the cathedral church, it is not out of keeping that the wall of the præhistoric *arx* should become the wall of the cathedral close. This is the wall which we see from afar, a wall which seems so straight and regular, so clearly furnished with a modern finish at top, that it is not till we can distinguish the mighty blocks of which it is formed that it has the air of a wall even of Roman, even of mediæval, antiquity. Shall we say it? As we looked up at no very amazing distance, the wall of the *arx* of Alatri had a good deal of the air of the wall of a modern prison. We could not yet see the construction, and the outline seemed more regular and rectangular than it proves to be. Nowhere do we better see than at Alatri the nature of these primitive walls. They are seldom walls in the same sense as the later walls of Rome or of other places, walls built on the ground and standing up clear on both sides. Their business commonly is, as is perhaps more clear at Alatri than anywhere else, to strengthen by masonry the scarped side of a hill. Hence they have little or no height within, and the gateways are necessarily reached from within by a steep descent. The open space at Alatri allows this arrangement to be studied with unusual ease. The wall is eminently a wall against a hill, and its arrangements are made with no small art. The weak corner has its double defence; the way up from the town at this point is carefully sheltered. And what stones they are with which the hill of Alatri is strengthened; above all, what stones they are which are piled together to form its main gateway. Nowhere indeed in the walls of Alatri, whether of temple, *arx*, or city, do we find anything quite so rude as the rudest part of the wall of Cori. All the stones, of whatever shape—and they are of many shapes—have clearly been cut; they are all laid according to some kind of system, though the system according to which they are laid is not the same in every part of the wall. In some parts they seem almost to take the shape of constructive arches, at least of attempts at arches, such as may be seen in gateways and roofs at Segni and elsewhere. The true arch, it is hardly needful to say, is nowhere found in the original work; nor do we find even any of the attempts at the arch in that position where we should have most naturally looked for them, in the gateways. The great gateway of the *arx* at Alatri is indeed a wonderful work. Its builders either knew the arch and despised it, or else the thought of the arch had not come into their heads. It is as pure an example of the lintel-construction as any gateway at Athens or Mykênê. We suppose that the lintel-stone of the great treasury is yet vaster than the huge lintel-stone at Alatri; but the Anakim of Alatri were at least rivals whom those of Mykênê could not have despised. But, except in vastness of construction, we must not compare the gateway at Alatri, perfectly plain, a mere piling, though a very skilful piling, of huge blocks with the really artistic work of the Mykênaian treasuries. It goes rather with the lion-gate; only there are no lions. The builders of Alatri could carve, as is shown over one of the smaller gateways of the *arx*. But they chose to carve quite other subjects than lions. On the great gate however they carved nothing; that is left in the stern majesty of the vast blocks which form it. And here we may distinguish between the cut blocks of the gateway itself and the far ruder blocks just within it, which merely formed part of the foundation, and which, when the steep path went down to the gate, would not have stood above ground. Even the builders of primæval walls clearly drew a line between what was meant to meet the public eye and what was not.

But we must remember that the walls of which we have been speaking, the walls which first catch the eye, are not the whole of the walls of Alatri. They fence in only its inner and higher circuit. Their effect in the distant view is so imposing that the visitor will most likely be tempted to go to them first, instead of doing things in a more regular order by first tracking out the walls of the town itself. But these last, except that they do not supply anything like the primæval gate, are just as well worthy of study as the walls of the *arx* itself. They remain perfectly round the greater part of the circuit of the city, and they are of the same general construction as the walls of the *arx*. At some points a singular contrast is made by mediæval additions to the defences; good thirteenth century work, with the characteristic windows of the time, stands out as projections from the primæval wall. And, as in some of the other places, we have something thrown in in the way of what the walls contain, besides the attractions of the walls themselves. From the *arx* of Alatri we look down on several bell-towers and rose-windows, and one church at least, that of *Santa Maria Maggiore*, though hardly equal to its namesake at Ferentino, is quite worthy of examination. But, next to its walls, the strong point of Alatri lies in its domestic buildings. Very seldom, in Italy or out of it, do we see graceful windows, chiefly couplets with a divided shaft, more thickly gathered together, than in its crooked and narrow streets. Alatri, in short, is, to the antiquarian eye, satisfactory in every point save one. There should have been some decent building, pagan or Christian, crowning the noble site of its *arx*, the noblest in our whole range.

With Alatri we end one main stage of our *iter*, that of the hill-cities. We shall henceforth pass by places which lie more in the world, some of them in the thick of modern communication. But if we had turned back at Alatri, we should have done a good stroke of work. A journey to the walls of the Hernicans is in every way pleasant and profitable. And in truth, even if we throw in the Old-Latins and the Volscians, it is not a journey of hardships. The little inns are very humble, very simple, but they may be fed in and slept in without anything very frightful to endure. It may perhaps be well to mention that the *Locanda d'Italia*, at Anagni, recommended in various guide-books, has ceased to exist for some years. Still a day and a night at Anagni are no hardship, and a guide may be found, shirtless and letterless, who knows what is really worth going to much better than many in England who boast at once more clothes and more learning. Indeed, the men of the walls seem altogether a kindly and well-disposed race. Some say that is because they are said to be reclaimed brigands, perhaps on the principle that a reformed rake used to be said to make the best husband. There are indeed more beggars among them than need be; but on this head a wise rule was laid down by a young Volscian, or he might be a Hernican—we cannot always be exact among these obsolete nationalities—"Give to the halt and the blind; but not to anybody else."

IV. FROM ALATRI TO CAPUA.

We have done for a while with the hill-cities, though it would not be hard to find several other spots of the same kind, rivalling in historical interest, and, by all accounts, rivalling also as to existing remains, any of those which we have gone through. But the special necessities of an *iter ad Brundisium* carry us to quite other parts of the Italian peninsula, to parts where the sources of interest are fully equal to those of Etruscan or Latin cities, but where they are wholly different in kind. We leave the hills, or touch only their lowest slopes. For a while the mountains still soar above us, while our work is in the plains. Presently we lose the mountains even as distant companions; but before long we have the blue waves of Hadria as their substitute. At last we reach our goal; we go for a season even beyond it. And when we have gone as far as the devices of modern science can carry us, when we have reached the very end of the general railway system of Central Europe, our landscape again takes in both the sea and the mountains. But the eye now ranges beyond the bounds of Italy, beyond the bounds of Western Europe. We see across the narrowed waters to the heights of another peninsula. Without seeking for more than a chance likeness between the names—a name that ranges from the Euxine to the Hudson—without seeking in any sort to identify the Ἀλβανοί of Dionysios and the Ἀλβανοί of imperial Anna, it is still with a curious feeling of coincidence that the eyes which not many days before were looking up to the mount of Alba, now look across the sea to the wilder mountains of Albania.

Some of those who now looked across had already learned something of those heights from earlier and nearer experiences. Still it is a new feeling to look out on them from Italian ground, above all to look out on them from the spot where the Turk made his entrance into the western world, and where the signs of his short presence have stamped themselves deep on local memory. Standing at Otranto, looking on the Albanian heights, the foremost thought is how near Otranto came to being to the West of Europe all that the Thracian Kallipolis was to the East. But we are as yet far from Otranto, far from the heel of the boot, far even from any point of the Hadriatic coast. We are still on the western side of the great backbone of Italy; we have still to catch glimpses of the Tyrrhenian waters, to look, as at distant objects, on the bold outline of Ischia and on Vesuvius crowned with his pillar of cloud. But this time we do not obey the seemingly inflexible law which decrees that he who goes to Rome and does not turn back from

Rome must go and see Naples, whether he dies after the sight or not. This time we have no call either to Naples itself or to the far more attractive range of objects of which Naples is the centre. Our errand is to pass from the primæval cities of the Latin and the Volscian to the cities of south-eastern Italy. Their chief present attraction lies in the series of churches raised in the days of the Norman and Angevin kings; but their memories carry us back through a long series of stirring ages, not indeed to the hoary antiquity of Cori and Alatri, but to the days when Southern Italy, the earliest Italy, was counted for a part of Hellas. It is not for nothing that we look out from thence on those eastern lands which then perhaps were the less Hellenic of the two.

Greek influence indeed begins—some say that it historically began—on the western, not the eastern, shore of Italy, in lands which, in the present journey, we leave to the west of us and see only in glimpses. We hurry on, passing by much that we might well stop and study, from Frosinone to Caserta. And we are luxurious enough to rejoice at finding ourselves there. We have proved that a few days and nights may be passed among Volscians and Hernicans without damage or even serious discomfort; but we trust that it is not an avowal to be ashamed of that it is a pleasing exchange to find ourselves in thoroughly civilized quarters in the plains of Campania. We have found our Capua; not, however, at Capua itself, but under the shadow of the royal palace a few miles off. But we desert Capua only because Capuan comforts—we will not talk of luxuries—have fled from Capua and have found their new home at Caserta. Those who have tried a night at Capua itself, *Santa Maria di vetere Capua*, not the newer Capua on the site of Casilinum, report that, if Hannibal's army could be quartered there again, they would certainly not be corrupted by anything excessive in the way of creature comforts. Anagni and Frosinone are said to be far in advance of the city which long was to Rome what Paris long was to London. The excuse doubtless would be that Capua is Capua no longer. The name of Capua, and with it the stirring history of early mediæval Capua, has wandered from the true Capua to Casilinum. It is not at the town now called Capua, but at the village—it is hardly more—of Santa Maria, that we must look for what is left of Etruscan Vulturnum, of Samnite, Campanian, and Roman Capua, the special city of pleasure, the city where, before all others, pleasure was sought for in scenes of blood.

On our present course we have no special call to either Capua, old or new. We have in times past seen both the amphitheatre of the elder Capua and the cathedral portico of the newer. But, when Caserta has been chosen as a convenient halting-place, it would be a shame for the historic traveller to pass by two such famous spots without a glance at either, while in their neighbourhood lies a third object, of no small value in its own line, which will have the further charm of novelty. It is well, while still fresh from the Flavian amphitheatre at Rome, to look again on the amphitheatre of Capua—Capua, the mistress of Rome in the sports of slaughter. There is a certain special lore of amphitheatres, the mastery of which does not fall to the lot of all, even of those who look on the monuments either of Rome or Capua with a general historical eye. But it is easy to see that in the Capuan amphitheatre the underground arrangements can be studied as they hardly can be studied anywhere else. The walls, the seats, are far less perfect than at Rome; much more then are they less perfect than at Verona. But the substructure seems wholly untouched. In the Roman Coliseum the underground work is only partially brought to light, while of what has been brought to light it is not always clear how much is the work of the Flavian Emperors, and how much of the mediæval barons who turned the amphitheatre into a fortress. Here, better than at Rome, we may study what really happened when the lions came up from underground to be slaughtered by the imperial hands of Commodus. If any question is raised as to the date of the building, one who is not a special Capuan topographer may be satisfied with the fact, that the inscription of Hadrian claims for that prince only a renovation and enrichment of the building with columns and statues. This seems to imply that the shell is older; it may be far older. In idea at least, the amphitheatre of Capua is far older than that of Rome. It illustrates a strange but well-known law of human nature, that the taste for luxury and the taste for blood should find a common home.

Besides the modernized basilica, besides the tombs of various sizes and designs which line the road—one of which is indeed singularly like a model of an amphitheatre—the true Capua has little to show besides the amphitheatre itself. It is strange to see so great a city, one which for some ages must have been far greater, far more splendid than Rome, so utterly gone—or rather to see the little that is left of it translated to another site. But great as Capua undoubtedly was, we begin to doubt its extreme antiquity. Capua, once Etruscan Vulturnum, remained Etruscan Vulturnum till the fourth century of Rome. It was the last remnant of the great Etruscan dominion in that region of Italy. As such, it represents a state of things far older than Rome. But the city itself may well be of later date than Rome. At all events, we may be sure that it is of far later date than Cori and Alatri. The city by the Vulturnus, down in the plain, taking its name from its guardian river, marks an advance not only on the mountain strongholds of Segni and Norba, but on Veii, on Rome itself. It must be far older than Florence; but it is the fellow of Florence; it marks an equal forsaking of the oldest type of a city. It is hard to see where the *arx* of Capua could have stood, if we are to understand by an *arx* something set upon a hill. But what a position that of Capua was, according to later ideas, is shown by its revival after the Hannibalian war. The Samnite settlement, parted away from their kinsfolk of the mountains, had become Campanians, and, to seek shelter against their kinsfolk of the mountains, they had been fain in some sort to become Romans.

"Cives Romani tunc facti sunt Campani,"

says the line which comes as such a relief after the involved constructions of later Latin writers, a line which records a fact as simply worded as it could be in a mediæval chronicle, which gives us a true leonine rime, and which makes its way through six feet without a single dactyl. To the Campanian knights their Roman citizenship was doubtless pleasant enough; it may have been less so to the commons, who had the private rights only, and who were burthened with a payment to the knights. Yet we find that the revolt of Capua to Hannibal was largely the work of noble leaders. The truth doubtless is that the large amount of independence which Capua still kept only made any measure of dependence more galling. Then came the blow which made Capua for a while cease to be a city. Its lands became the property of the Roman people; its walls were left simply as a shelter for those who filled them. Yet the great city of Campania arose again, to be once more a great city till the second blow, when men of Semitic speech came not as deliverers but as destroyers, when Capua moved to Casilinum, and when all that was left of the elder city put itself under the keeping of a heavenly protectress as Santa Maria di Capua. Among those remnants of what was, the walls of Capua, the *arx* of Capua, are not to be found; at all events they do not strike the traveller on his first or his second visit. For something faintly answering to a Capuan *arx*, he takes himself to the neighbouring mountains. There, on their lowest slopes, looking out on Vesuvius and Ischia, looking down on the Campanian plain, with its river, with its older and its newer Capua, we come to a spot where a famous temple of the older faith has given way to a less famous one of the new. A journey from Caserta to the Capuan amphitheatre in the plain may well take in a journey to the slope of Tifata, the slope of the hill on which Hannibal so often pitched his camp, and where the church of Sant' Angelo in Formis has supplanted the holy place of Diana and Jupiter, which took its name from the mountain which rises above its massy tower.

V. A CHURCH BY THE CAMP OF HANNIBAL.

We reach Tifata, the very centre of the marching and counter-marching of Hannibal, the spot from which we may best call up a picture of beleaguered Capua, of Fulvius waiting for his prey, of the stout fighting on either side of the enclosing lines, of Hannibal, as his last hope, turning aside to threaten Rome, in the chance that the danger of Rome might lead to the relief of Capua. The name Tifata, in some tongue, most likely in the old Oscan, describes the evergreen oaks which doubtless formed the sacred grove of Diana. The goddess had no lake here, as she had at Aricia, nor do we hear of any such grim legend on Tifata as grew round—

Those trees in whose dim shadow

   The ghastly priest doth reign,

The priest who slew the slayer,

   And shall himself be slain.

Yet beside the rites of Canaan, the rites of the gods who had sent forth him whose name proclaimed him as the Grace of Baal, the darkest forms into which any kind of Italian or Hellenic worship strayed might well seem mild. In tracking the career of Hannibal, we are ever disappointed at the utter lack of means to call up a picture of the man himself apart from his public acts. He had human weaknesses, for he found a mistress at Salapia. He had his sallies of merriment, for he could raise a laugh at the grave Gisgo. But the course of his inner life is hidden from us. Still we can at least see that he was, in his own belief, charged with a mission from the gods of his own city. And it needs an effort to bear in mind that the gods of Hannibal were Baal and Moloch. The goddess to whom he would have reared a temple would have been, not a Diana, but an Ashtoreth. Yet, among the many, and mostly false, charges of cruelty brought against the great Phœnician by Roman writers, we do not hear, as we do in the case of some other Carthaginian commanders, of captives being made to pass through the fire to the gods of Carthage. Hannibal, the friend of Capua, would at Capua honour Diana of Tifata; but it was not Diana that had sent him. With what thanks did he honour his own gods, when Capua, second city of all Italy, welcomed the victor of Trebia, Trasimenus, and Cannæ? Is it too bold a flight to fancy the mount of Tifata the scene of the same form of Baal-worship as the mount of Carmel?

But the gods of Italy lived on, undisturbed by the momentary presence of Semitic rivals. Diana was not the only power worshipped on Tifata; Jupiter also had his holy place. And it may be that the venerable church which now forms the chief attraction of the hill-side represents the holy place of Jupiter rather than the holy place of Diana. It is curious to see how a kind of appropriateness was often sought after in the nomenclature of Pagan temples when turned into Christian churches. Thus, at Athens, the Parthenôn remained the Parthenôn, while the temple of the warrior Thêseus or Hêraklês became the church of the warrior George. We should look for a *Santa Maria* or a *Santa Lucia* at the least, on the site of the sanctuary of Diana. Had we here a *San Pietro*, we should have very little doubt in setting down the prince of the Apostles as having supplanted the father of gods and men. But at *Sant' Angelo in Formis* we feel somewhat less certain; St. Michael suggests the Norman, and the Norman has been there. It may well be that the name is no older than his day.

But St. Michael on the slope of Tifata did carry us back in thought to a church of St. Peter seen some months before under a widely different state of outward things. We then made a somewhat difficult journey to a great and solitary Tuscan basilica in time of snow. The outward aspect of nature had certainly changed a good deal between the bleak day in January when it was found a hard task to follow the way from Pisa to the basilica of the prince of the Apostles *in Grado* and the sunny day in May when the same travellers found their way without difficulties of any kind to the basilica of the prince of the archangels *in Formis*. And there certainly can be no likeness of position, even if both were seen in January or both in May, between the basilica standing low in the flats by the mouth of Arno and the basilica which nestles against the mountains which form a wall to the rich plain of Vulturnus. But in seeing any one of these great churches, left, not ruined, like our Cistercian abbeys, but still living on a kind of life in places forsaken or nearly so, something always brings up the memory of some other of its fellows. Aquileia is perhaps the greatest case of all; but Aquileia, with its special position in the history of the world, stands by itself. If Aquileia itself is dead, it has lived on a wonderful after-life in the shape of its Venetian colony. We go to see Aquileia, because it is Aquileia; but even a well-informed traveller may know nothing of *San Pietro in Grado* and *Sant' Angelo in Formis*, till either his guide-book or some earlier visitor points them out to him as places which he ought not to pass by. Aquileia again has other things to show besides the great basilica and its surroundings. St. Apollinaris *in Classe* is as nearly forsaken as a church that is still kept up can be; but the basilica of Classis does not stand by itself; it forms part of the wonders of Ravenna, as St. Paul without-the-Walls forms part of the wonders of Rome. St. Peter *in Grado* might be looked on as standing in the same relation to Pisa; but it hardly enters into our general conception of

Pisa, as the church of Classis—papal havoc hinders us from adding the church of Cæsarea—certainly enters into our general conception of Ravenna. S. Angelo *in Formis* at all events does not enter into our general conception of old Capua, because there is not enough of old Capua left to form any general conception of it at all. The church and the small surrounding village do form a kind of distant *arx* to the greater collection of houses which surrounds the amphitheatre; but among the nearer objects which catch the eye from the height, the most prominent is not old Capua with its amphitheatre, but new Capua, Casilinum that once was, with its towers and cupolas, mediæval and modern. We look on many things from the terrace in front of the portico of the archangel, but that which among artificial objects chiefly draws the eye towards it, is not the elder Capua of Hannibal and Marcellus, but the Capua which succeeded Aversa as the seat of the elder but the less famous of the Norman powers in Southern Italy. As we mark the advance of national union, no less than as we mark the advance of mere dynastic aggression, we have sometimes to think, for a moment perhaps to mourn, that "kingdoms have shrunk to provinces," though in this form of advance and incorporation, we have no longer to add that "chains clank over sceptred cities." Capua, on both its sites, once the head of an Etruscan, once of a Norman dominion, passed, in one age, under the universal rule of Rome. In another age it again sank from its separate headship to become a member of that greater Norman dominion in Apulia and Sicily which, after more shiftings, unions, divisions, transfers to distant rulers, than any other part of Europe, has in our days been merged in the realm of united Italy, with Rome as its head, but not its mistress.

We reach then the height which, whether that of Jupiter or Diana of old, is now the height of the warrior archangel. The whole history of the church belongs to the independent days of the second Capua; in its present shape it belongs to the days of independent Norman rule in the second Capua. But the days of independent Norman rule were days when the arts of the earlier rulers of the land still lived on. We see signs of the art of Byzantium, so long mistress of Southern Italy, and of the art of the Saracen, in Italy only a visitor or an invader, while in Sicily an abiding master. The portico in front of the church is Roman in its general idea; but, instead of the colonnade and entablature of the Laurentian basilica, we see an arcade whose pointed arches at once call up memories of Sicily. They have indeed little of Sicilian grace. Nowhere at Palermo or Monreale do we see such massive columns bearing such massive stilts. Columns indeed we should hardly say, as some of them are plainly mere fragments. But here, just as in Sicily, just as in Aquitaine, the pointed arch is no sign of coming Gothic; the style is still wholly Romanesque, and somewhat rude Romanesque too. And in this region of Italy we can hardly doubt as to attributing the almost accidental shape of the arches to the influence of Saracen models, perhaps to the workmanship of Saracen craftsmen. Hard by, but not joining the building, by an arrangement unlike Sicily, unlike Apulia, but the common rule of Northern Italy, rises a bell-tower, or rather the beginning of a bell-tower, which raises our wonder as to what it would have been if it had ever grown to its full height. Two stages only are finished, the lower of hewn stone, the upper of brick; but their bulk is so great that the tower, if it had ever been finished, would surely have ranked among the highest of its class, utterly overpowering even the great basilica at its side, except so far as it would have been itself overpowered by the natural heights above it. As in some other cases, the thought suggests itself, were not those who left off building the tower wiser than those who began it? The tall bell-towers of Italy look well as they rise from the Lombard plain, as they crown the hill of Fiesole, as they skirt the shores of the lake of Como. But we are not sure that a gigantic tower, which, if it was to have any kind of proportion, ought to have been carried up to a height as great as that of Venice, was in its right place when set a little way up a mountain-side, as if simply to show how small man's biggest works look in the midst of the works of nature. But the technical eye is thankful for the fragment that has been built, though mainly on a very technical ground. Professor Willis is gone, but his happy phrase of *mid-wall* shafts has not died with him. The custom of the elder Romanesque towers, the abiding fashion of Germany and Northern Italy, was to set the little columns which divided the coupled windows in the very middle of the wall; the latter Norman fashion, whether in Normandy, in England, or in Apulia, was to set them nearly flush with the outer wall. In this tower, Italian by geography, Norman by allegiance, two sides conform to the Italian and two to the Norman fashion. Nothing can show more clearly that even such small matters of detail as the use of a mid-wall shaft were made matters of serious thought, and that it was sometimes thought well to come to a compromise between two rival forms of taste.

The outside of this church, except so far as it forms an object in the general landscape, is perhaps chiefly attractive to the technical observer; the inside will surely appeal to every visitor, though the visitor who is technically informed in matters of painting may possibly look upon it with more of curiosity than of positive admiration. But the eye of the more general inquirer will give something like positive admiration to a basilica of eight arches, resting on ancient columns of various marbles, with its original design far less damaged than is common in Italian churches, and with every inch of available space covered with elaborate paintings of the date of the building. Like St. Peter by Pisa, the archangel by Capua trusted to painting for his enrichment and not to mosaics; and though the Campanian pictures are by far the better preserved of the two, though nearly all the subjects can be made out with the greatest ease, yet Ravenna and Venice rise to the mind to make us think that at least if endurance be the object, there is a more excellent way.

The walls of this church form almost a pictorial Bible, with a few legendary and local subjects thrown in. The Abbot Desiderius, holding, after the usual symbolical fashion, the church in his hand, is to be seen at the east end along with the archangels and evangelists. At the west end is what connoisseurs tell us is one of the very earliest pictures of the Last Judgment. On the two sides a crowd of scenes and figures from the Old and New Testament cover the whole space. The style of the painting is said to show Greek workmanship; we look toward the west end and mark, hardly above the ground, a single small shaft with a capital of strictly Byzantine character. The ruling Norman seems on this spot to have pressed into his service the artistic powers of all the inhabitants of the peninsula. Italian, Greek, Saracen, all give their help to adorn the house of the archangel. The Norman himself contributes nothing but the position of two small columns in the tower windows. We cannot even attribute to him the position of the house of the archangel, set Norman-fashion in a high place; for the first church was built before the Norman came. It is not so further east, where a distinctively Norman element is to be seen in the great churches of Apulia. But the gathering together of the best skill of the time from all quarters is a thoroughly Norman function, whether in Italy or in England.

The basilica should be compassed, so far at least as to climb the hill a little way to look at its east end. Its surrounding buildings supply an arch or two to catch the eye on the way up or down. But the essential features of Sant' Angelo are the grand display of painting and the union of elements of so many kinds. It is the first of a great series of churches at which our course will bid us to stop here and there. But before we reach them we shall pass by one point where our musings will again be mainly secular and largely pagan. A short journey will lead us from Campania into Samnium, and the valiant men of the Samnite land will claim a tribute on a spot which is Samnite beyond all others.

VI. A GLIMPSE OF SAMNIUM.

From Caserta and what is to be seen from Caserta, our next journey lies by the line of railway which runs right across Italy, connecting the two great lines of the east and west of the peninsula. It leads us from the Campanian plain, with at least its sheltering wall of mountains, with Tifata to guard the great city that once was from the ruder land beyond, to the great plain of Apulia from which every feature of a mountain-land has passed away. But, in so crossing from one side of Italy to the other, we pass through a striking and an historic region. We are in the land of the mightiest Italian rivals of Rome, the land of those with whom Rome had to fight, before Pyrrhos and Hannibal came, and ages after Pyrrhos and Hannibal were gone.

Our course leads us into the heart of the Samnite land, a land which may well call up endless musings on the hard fate of those "hearts of steel" who bore up so long against Rome, in the days when Rome was really at her greatest. And the memories of the same land in after days are not wholly alien to those of earlier times. Our course brings us, at not a few points, across the memories, if not of nations, yet of men, who had to bear up against the power of Rome, when the power of Rome had taken a far other form than that of the senate and the armies against which the Samnite had to strive. For the old Samnite land holds its place in later story, as the land of princes who felt what the spiritual Rome could do when the powers of the spiritual Rome were at their highest. We pass through regions which were the scene of no small part of the history of the Norman and Swabian lords of Sicily and Southern Italy. We are deep in the land of the counts, dukes, kings, and emperors of the house of Hauteville and the house of Hohenstaufen; and we are often called on to stop and track out their deeds. At not a few points do we light on some building, some inscription, which brings up the memory of Frederick, the Wonder of the World, and of Manfred, whose field of overthrow we shall presently pass by. In both periods the history of these lands has a character altogether different from that of Northern and Central Italy. In the later period this needs no proof: we are dealing with the history of a kingdom, not with the history of a system of separate cities. But something of the same difference extends to the earlier period also. If we wish to know more of Volscians and Hernicans, yet more keenly do we wish to know more of Samnites. The part which they played is greater, at all events in scale, and their dealings with Rome belong to a stage of Roman history when we feel that we have a kind of right to know more than we could hope to know in the earlier time.

But while we know something of the character of the Samnite people as a whole, while we know something—though much less than in some other Italian lands—of the geography of the Samnite country, we have no clear notion of the political position or the political action of any particular Samnite city or canton, such as we ever and anon do get of particular cities of Etruria and Latium. And again, it is seldom that we can call up any distinct personal conception of any Samnite leader as a living and breathing man. This is indeed a grievance which affects Samnites along with the other Italian enemies of Rome. The personal conceptions which we do get of Etruscans and Latins largely belong to legendary times. Of historical Volscians we know very few. And we have already complained on Hernican ground that we cannot picture to ourselves the personal likeness of any single Hernican of independent Hernican days.

Still, on this particular journey we have small right to complain; for we pass by the spot which calls up the memories of the most memorable Samnites of whom we have any personal knowledge. They are men of one name, most likely therefore of one house, and men of whom we emphatically wish to know more than we do know. Leaving Caserta behind, glancing at the Campanian plain and the Campanian mountains, marking Naples only by the smoke of the distant city, we pass along through what, in our simplicity, we take to be the vale of Vulturnus, till we light on a more classical friend, armed with a more classical map, who explains that the stream which we are tracing is in strictness not Vulturnus himself, but only his tributary Calor. Anyhow we go along its course into the heart of the Samnite land, and we pass by one spot—a spot which we ought to have treated better than merely to pass it by, a spot round which the greatest memories of Samnite history gather, and where they strangely interweave themselves with wholly different memories of the history of our own land. We reach Telesia, the home of the Pontii, and we remember that Telesia was also for a moment the home of Anselm. Our guide-book provokingly fails us; but the large building on the hill-side must surely be the monastery where he sojourned. There are Roman antiquities in the place; for Samnite antiquities we do not look. But did Samnites build no walls, or do the mighty bulwarks of Cori and Segni mark an earlier state of things than the Sabellian occupation of Southern Italy? Anyhow, we are here at the place which has attached itself as a surname to the two most memorable men in the scanty personal history of Samnium. Here, on his own ground, we remember that Gaius Pontius who spared Rome's army at the Caudine Forks, and who lived to be led, twenty-seven years later, as a spectacle in a Roman triumph, to end his days, one might almost say as a martyr, by the axe of the headsman in a Roman dungeon. So we used to read the tale in our youth; so moralized the historians of our youth over the special baseness which handed over such a man to such an end. Or are we to adopt the new reading of the tale which at least saves Quintus Fabius Maximus from that special stain of blood-guiltiness which cleaves to the canonized memory of Divus Julius? It may be well if we can believe that one of the worthiest heroes of the old commonwealth, if he could not forestall the magnanimity of Pompeius and Aurelian, at least did not sink to the special and petty spite of the murderer of Vercingetorix. We are now taught that the Gaius Pontius who appears twenty-seven years after the first mention of that name, is most likely not the same man as the merciful victor of the Caudine Forks. If this be so, then Quintus Fabius, in consigning his Pontius to the axe, merely conformed to the cruel custom of his nation, without the further aggravation of slaying in cold blood one who had dealt with Rome so nobly. And after all some might hint that the oldest Pontius of all was the wisest. It may be that the sage old father of Gaius knew human nature best, when he bade his son either to massacre the whole Roman army or else to let them go free without terms. It may be that the son chose a more dangerous path than either, when he took to diplomacy and middle courses.

But if the earlier Pontius of Telesia should prove—though the guess is a simple guess—to be in truth two Pontii, perhaps a father and a son, no doubt seems to have fixed itself on the identity of the last Pontius at the Colline gate of Rome. The rising again of Samnite life at the last moment of all, when the war with the allies seemed to have lost itself in the deeper whirlpool of the war of Marius and Sulla, is really the most striking thing in the whole history, such as we have it, of the Samnite people. We are taken by surprise when, in days when Rome already seems the fully established head, not only of Italy, but of all the Mediterranean world, her power, her very being, is threatened by the leader of a nation which seemed to have been dead and buried for some centuries. But, just like the Volumnian tomb in one way, so the Samnite resurrection in another way is a witness to the real life which the other states of Italy kept on under a form of Roman dominion which made them externally dependent, which threw its influence into the scale of oligarchy in their external affairs, which ever and anon subjected them to some irregular demand, but which left the general course of their lives to be whatever they themselves chose it to be. In the days of Marius and Sulla, Etruscans and Samnites were still Etruscans and Samnites; they had not become Romans, nor had they merged their being in any common name of Italians. The Social War itself was the first attempt at forming a general Italian nationality. But the last campaign of the last Pontius shows how deep, in Samnite hearts at least, was the earlier feeling, the feeling which knew no greater whole than the federal union of Etruria or Samnium. It shows too how specially deep was the feeling of hatred for the single city which had brought down so many cities and leagues to become its helpless dependents. Against Pontius at the Colline gate Rome fought for life, as she had never fought since the old days when she had to guard herself against enemies who lived within sight of her capitol. Foreign invaders, Pyrrhos, Hannibal himself, did not come with the same fixed purpose of rooting up the wood which sheltered the wolves of Italy. We can hardly doubt that it is the hand of Sulla which from that day to this has hindered the south of Italy from being like the north. But the blow which crushed the Samnite people as the other nations of Italy were not crushed, was vengeance taken for a moment when it once more became a question whether Rome should rule over Italy, whether Rome should exist at all.

At Telesia we look out, and muse on what might have been, if one Pontius had done otherwise than he did by the forks of Caudium, if another Pontius had fared otherwise than he fared at the gates of Rome herself. At our next halting-place we are called on, not to muse on what might have been, but on what was. At Beneventum we tread the battle-ground of Pyrrhos and Manfred, the ground of two of the greatest victories of the Rome of the earlier and the Rome of the later day. There we need not strive to call up the dim figures of men, like the older and the later Pontius, known by one action of their lives. The Epeirot and the Swabian stand out as clearly discerned figures in the history of their several ages. And the places where we next halt will show us the place of overthrow for both, the place of death and utter ruin for one.

VII. BENEVENTO.

We follow the stream of Calore till we reach a city which, without ever having been one of the great cities of the world, without having been even one of the greatest cities of Italy, has always kept up an important historic being. Beneventum is a familiar name in all ages; yet Beneventum has never been either a mighty commonwealth like Venice or Genoa, or the head of a mighty kingdom like Naples and Palermo. It has had its princes; if we never heard of them before, we should learn a good deal of them by studying the monuments of their city. That is to say, the monuments will tell us a great deal about princes nine hundred or a thousand years back; no monument that we remember in Benevento tells us anything about the last prince who bore their title. Let us suppose a wanderer who began his travels at Autun and who finds himself, in the course of the same wandering, at Benevento. He will feel it as a grotesque coincidence that, not so very long ago, a man was living who had once been Prince of Benevento and who before that had been Bishop of Autun. Benevento, among many other things that it is, is also the later city of Talleyrand, as Autun is the earlier. But there is this difference that one thinks of Talleyrand at Autun and one does not think of him at Benevento. At Autun he has his place, though a very strange place, in the long succession of Bishops of Autun; at Benevento, though he bore the style of its prince, he stands all alone; we cannot find a niche for him in the succession of the Beneventan princes. Yet a prince of Benevento whose existence marks the ending for a season of the long papal dominion in Benevento reminds us that Benevento had its princes before that papal dominion began. It reminds us of the two distinctive features in the later history of the city. Benevento was first the seat of Lombard princes who, placed on the borders of both empires, contrived to escape all practical submission to either; it was then the seat of an outlying scrap of papal dominion surrounded on all sides by the Sicilian realm. In both these characters Benevento was a kind of curiosity on the historical map of Europe. But the city had its ups and downs before those days, and amongst other things it had gone through a somewhat grotesque change of name. It is hard to believe that a city placed so far inland can really have been of Greek origin; but legend attributed it to a Greek founder, and its oldest name had a Greek sound. Greek *Maloeis*, Samnite *Maluentum*, had, when it was read into Latin *Maloventum*, an ill sound; so, when the Samnite stronghold was changed into the Roman colony, it took the name of Beneventum, city of welcome.

Beneventum, marked by Procopius as a strong city in a high place, stands low as compared with the true hill-cities. Still, as compared with Capua, it might itself pass for a hill-city. It has just that amount of rise above the river which there commonly is where there is a river, such a rise as may be seen in many an English town which is not as Durham or Lincoln. We miss the primæval walls of the hill-cities; but we find, on the other hand, works of Roman and mediæval art such as in the hill-cities we do not find. The arch of Trajan has vanished from Rome, except so far as it lives in the sculptures which were torn from it to enrich the arch of Constantine. But at Benevento, as at Ancona, the memorial of the conqueror of Dacia still abides. The Beneventan arch may indeed fairly take its place in the Roman series. It belongs essentially to the same class of designs as the arch of Severus and the arch of Constantine, while it has little in common with its own tall and slender fellow at Ancona. At the same time, since it has, in general effect at least, taken upon itself something of the position of a town-gate, since it bears the name of *Porta aurea*, to match the golden gate of Constantinople and the golden gate of Spalato, the arch of Beneventum has now a somewhat greater air of reality than triumphal arches commonly have. The weak point of that class of structures is that they are of no use. They do not, like a wall, a gateway, a house, a temple, a hall of council, serve any purpose in the ordinary economy of things. They are purely monumental, set up to commemorate something or somebody, but in no way to help on men's daily affairs, public or private. And yet they are not mere monuments, like a statue or an inscribed stone. A large building of this kind, having very much the air of a building which does serve some purpose, is a little deceptive. It is so like a real gateway that it calls up the thought of a real gateway, and leaves us a little disappointed at finding that the building, after all, never was of any use to anybody, and was set up simply to be looked at. There is, therefore, something a little unsatisfactory in the whole class of triumphal arches, and it may even be that a slightly ludicrous element is thrown in when we find that the immediate occasion for rearing this record of the life and exploits of the "fortissimus princeps" whom it commemorates was the repair of the Appian Way. But it does not become us to find fault with any built and graven monument, specially with one of a time of which we have so few written monuments as the memorable reign of Trajan. We are so much the slaves of accidental associations, so apt to draw lines at some altogether unreasonable point, that we may doubt whether the reign of Trajan holds the place which it should hold in popular imagination. Suetonius wrote the lives of Twelve Cæsars, and this mere accident has caused the notion of a break which has no real existence between the Suetonian Twelve and those who next followed them. The reign of Trajan marks the Empire at its highest pitch of extent and power, at that highest pitch which, in its own nature, comes just before the beginning of decay. His days saw, too, the highest pitch of architectural magnificence; and with Tacitus and Juvenal to adorn it, one might be inclined to say that, as an age of Latin literature, the age of Trajan might hold its own against any earlier period of the Imperial rule. For we must remember that the great writers of the early days of Augustus are in truth writers of the republican period living on into the Empire. The Flavian period, continued under Trajan, is quite as rich as the earlier days of the Empire itself. And we may notice that the arch of Beneventum marks the reign of Trajan, and with it the Roman Empire, at what was really its highest point. It was raised at a time when it could commemorate conquered Dacia and tributary Armenia. That Dacia and Armenia could be brought within the range of that Roman world which is continued in the system of modern Europe is proved by daily witnesses. But the arch of Beneventum was built too early to commemorate its hero's later victories in the further East, momentary victories in lands which neither Alexander nor Trajan could bring within the abiding range of Western influences.

The arch of Trajan is so distinctly the most famous thing in Benevento that it has carried us out of all chronological order. But the historical interest of Beneventum lies earlier and later than Trajan's day. In truth the *Pax Romana* forbade that the main interest of any Italian city should lie in Trajan's day. We may believe or not as we please in the presence of Diomêdês and Æneas; but Pyrrhos, Hanno, Totilas, and Manfred are visitors who cannot be forgotten. The city has looked out on many battles, from the overthrow of the Molossian to the overthrow of the Swabian. A pleasing tale in its history is when that Tiberius Gracchus who is the first of a name to appear in Roman history led back his victorious slave-soldiers to receive the reward of freedom, and to be welcomed by the rejoicing people of the faithful colony. For among the Thirty Cities of those days, the Latin colony of Beneventum was not one of the laggard twelve, but one of the faithful eighteen that were ready to endure all hardships. In later warfare the city seems to have been less steadfast. It welcomed Belisarius, and in after days Totilas took it without any trouble, and if he destroyed the walls it was not out of revenge for any resistance on the part of its inhabitants, but for fear they should supply a post of defence for an imperial army. But the greatest day of Beneventum as an historical city comes later than Totilas and earlier than Manfred. The memory of that day may be studied in the chief remaining buildings in the city, the two greatest churches and the castle. The west front of the metropolitan church, a grand example of Italian Romanesque, is furthermore a perfect chronicle of local history. There we may read, built up into the wall, a crowd of monumental records of the Lombard princes of Beneventum, with their deeds, especially their dealings with the dangerous power of the Franks, set forth at length. The bronze doors are famous, with their long array of Scriptural subjects ending in a lesson in the ecclesiastical geography of the province, the figures of the Archbishop of Beneventum and his suffragans. The harmony of the front is a little marred by the single low and massive corner-tower; but the inscription sums up the history of Beneventum, political and physical, for some ages. The city was laid waste by the Emperor Frederick in 1229 and by an earthquake in 1688. The tower was built after the first overthrow in 1279; it was restored after the second in 1690. Destruction wrought by the elements would thus seem to be more easily repaired than destruction wrought by the hand of Cæsar. But it is somewhat strange to find Frederick, in his own belief a successor of Trajan, a follower of Trajan in Eastern conquests, branded as a destroyer in the city where Trajan's memory is cherished. But Frederick had to deal with a kind of power which Trajan knew not. The wrath of the later Emperor fell on a city which was too faithful to the Roman Bishop. The course of Trajan's rule was not likely to be interfered with either by the obscure chief of the persecuted Christian sect, or by any minister of the creed of which Trajan was himself chief Pontiff.

Within the church the repairs done after the earthquake have wrought a good deal of mischief. But we can still see the four ranges of columns of a mighty basilica which must once have taken its place among the noblest of its class. Their capitals are a little nondescript; but they do not offend the eye; if they were certified to be of Trajan's day, it would doubtless be the right thing to admire them. The ambones and the Easter-light are lovely work of the early fourteenth century, the days of a real *Renaissance*, truer than that which followed. The treasury is rich in vestments and other precious things; but the reader of Anselm's *Life* looks in vain for that specially gorgeous vestment which a Beneventan Archbishop of the eleventh century bore away from Canterbury in exchange for the arm of St. Bartholomew, and which made its wearer the most splendid object among the assembled fathers at Bari. If this missing garment carries our thoughts to England, the round church of St. Sophia—hexagonal in its inner range—carries us to the Eastern world, and reminds us that there was more than one line of successors of Trajan, and that Beneventum came under the influences of both. The cloister, with its amazing series of capitals, its birds, its elephants, its hunting scenes, may rank with those of Aosta and of Arles, of which that of Aosta can supply camels to match the Beneventan elephants. The castle dates only from Pope John the Twenty-second, far away at Avignon; we look perhaps more carefully at the older fragments built up in its walls and on the lion in front of it. With the lion in our thoughts we may look out for other beasts, graven or molten or abiding in their own relics. Procopius saw there the tusks of the Kalydonian boar, as in later times he might, either at Warwick or at Bristol, have seen the ribs of the dun cow. It is for palæontologists to say what it was that the

Beneventan antiquaries really showed him. Failing this natural wonder we go to pay our respects to another beast whose shape is due to man's device, in quite another part of the city. A rudely carved bovine animal, in which local patriotism sees the Samnite bull—the bull which, on the coins of revived Samnium, so proudly trampled down the Roman wolf—is now cruelly to be ruled as nothing better than a monument of intruding Apis-worship. We have less time to spend at Benevento than at some other cities; but the Roman arches and vaults of the strange building called *Quaranta Santi*, the grand Roman bridge below, must not be forgotten, and we must still give one more thought to the two mighty men whose hopes were shattered at Beneventum. Manfred fell with his faithful Saracens around him; Pyrrhos lived to fall by a meaner end at Argos; but Beneventum ended the real career of both. It is strange how the two were in some sort the converse of each other. Pyrrhos carried the Epeirot arms into Sicily and southern Italy; Manfred, lord of Sicily and southern Italy, established a Sicilian dominion on the coast of Epeiros. Korkyra, Corfu, the island which has seen every master except the Turk, formed part of the dominions of both alike. We leave Benevento for another city in which the East and the West of Europe, and a crowd of other elements besides, meet yet more closely than they do at Benevento. At Beneventum the eye of Horace began to be caught by the well-known mountains of Apulia; Procopius somewhat boldly speaks of inland Beneventum as being opposite to Dalmatia. The city which we take as our next chief goal, if not strictly opposite to Dalmatia, is so marked as being opposite to one Illyrian port as to have sent its name, so to speak, across the Hadriatic. We will not trouble ourselves to look out for Equotuticum, or to regale ourselves with either the bread or the water of Canusium. It is to the walls of Bari, fishy Bari, that we have to make our way; at Bari, Greek, Latin, Saracen, even Englishman, are all at home, and Bari is opposite to Antivari.

VIII. NORMAN BUILDINGS IN APULIA.

At Foggia the line of railway which crosses the Italian peninsula from Naples eastward joins the great European line which for the most part skirts the Western Hadriatic shore. From Rome itself the *iter ad Brundisium* is still made by way of Beneventum; for the great mass of mankind Bologna has in this matter supplanted Beneventum and Rome too. Our eastward course across the peninsula has done for us much the same as would be done by the like course across our own island. We have undergone the same change as if we had passed from Wales, Devonshire, or Cumberland, to Lincolnshire or East-Anglia. We need no longer look out for hill-cities, where the first element in such cities, the hills themselves, is not to be found. At Foggia we have not even the amount of hill which we have at Benevento. We are in the great Apulian plain, the plain so precious for sheep-feeding, and the occupation of which has more than once given rise to wars and treaties. Of Foggia itself many perhaps have never heard except as a railway junction. Yet Foggia has a history, and its history has monuments, though we can hardly put them on a level with the monuments and the history of Beneventum. The capital of Apulia, the representative of ancient Arpi, has a history in some respects the same as that of Beneventum, in some other respects its opposite. Both cities claimed Diomêdês as a founder, while Frederick the Second, a destroyer at Benevento, appears as a later founder at Foggia. One arch of his palace still remains, with an inscription telling us how under him Foggia became a royal and Imperial seat. There died his English Empress Isabel, on the splendour of whose passage on her way to her marriage our own historians are eloquent. Further than this, the monumental attractions of Foggia hardly go beyond what is left of its chief church. Of its front Gsell-fels, gives a somewhat ideal engraving, showing it, not as it is, but as it was before earthquakes and restorers after earthquakes had combined to mar it. It was—indeed, with all mutilations, it still is—a fine front of the later Italian Romanesque, with one of the rose or wheel windows which we must now look for wherever we go. More attractive perhaps is the crypt, with its four columns and capitals of singular beauty. They surely belong to the time of the Imperial patron of Foggia, marking as they do a kind of earlier and more healthy *Renaissance*, which, taking classical form as its general models, took them only as general models, and did not deem itself bound slavishly to copy every turn of a leaf or every section of a moulding. Such works of the carver's tool are akin to those noble coins of Frederick which seem ages in advance of anything that bore the image and superscription of his grandfather.

Foggia is however less likely to strike the traveller—at least the traveller who comes from the hill-towns by way of Capua and Benevento—by any remarkable store of ancient monuments, than as being the first to which he will come of a series of cities, most of which at once impress the visitor by their air of modern progress and prosperity. The heel of Italy, in its cities at least, certainly seems to be the very opposite to a decaying region, or even to a region which stands still. To be sure, the city whose name is the most familiar of all is something of an exception; Brindisi, notwithstanding its dealings with the whole world, is not as Bari or even as Trani. But most of the towns at which we tarry, or which we pass by, give quite a different impression. We cannot tarry at all. At Barletta we get only a glimpse of the Imperial colossus, and therefore we do not venture to hazard a guess whether it is Heraclius or any later prince whom it represents. Along this coast, any Cæsar of the East is in his place, if only as a memorial of the long, though half forgotten, time when Southern Italy bowed to the New Rome and not to the Old. But we do not let these earlier memories wholly shut out the thought of the later combat when the Horatii and Curiatii of legend found themselves multiplied by a process exactly opposite to decimation. The attractions of Trani are irresistible; a bell-tower rising as proudly over the waves as that of Spalato itself would force us to halt even if we knew nothing before of what church and city has to show us. The metropolitan church of Trani is certainly one of the very noblest examples of that singular mixture of Norman and more strictly Italian forms—not without a touch both of the Greek and the Saracen—which is the characteristic style of this region, the natural result of its political history. Strange, but striking in the extreme, is the effect of the east end of this church rising close above the sea; far more truly admirable is the effect of the inside, where the coupled columns of the Saracen have been boldly taught to act as the piers of the great arcades, and to bear up above them a massive triforium, which by itself would make us think ourselves in Normandy or England. All the churches of this district have a good deal of their strength underground, and the under-church of Trani is worthy of the building which it supports. The smaller church, All Saints', a charming little basilica with a portico of singular grace, as also several good pieces of domestic architecture, and the general effect of the tower skirted with its dark arcades, all join to make Trani a place which cannot be passed by, though no august form calls on us, as at Barletta, to tarry to pay Cæsar his due homage. But Trani has found something to be said for itself both by pen and by pencil in quite other company. An accident of later times gave it a right to rank, like Brindisi itself, among the Subject and Neighbour Lands of Venice. And Trani has peculiarities of its own. The main features of the style may be studied elsewhere. We long to see Barletta, to tarry to pay Cæsar his due. We long to stop at Bisceglia and Molfetta, of which we read attractive notices; but again we must pick and choose, and Bitonto is the only place on which we can qualify ourselves to speak at all at large, till we come to the head of the whole region at Bari.

Bitonto shares a station with San Spirito, but it lies further away from the railway, and that on the inland side, than most of the towns along this line. Its main interest is found in its cathedral church, which in some points prepares us for the buildings of Bari. First of all in point of wonder, though latest in point of date, is the treatment which it has undergone at the hands of modern improvers. A dim remembrance comes to us that we saw something of the same kind in the Dominican church at Perugia; otherwise we ask in amazement why any man should think it an improvement to cut off the whole upper part of a church as seen inside by thrusting in a roof a great deal lower than the original one, and thereby leaving the upper stages outside to stand up in the air, serving no kind of purpose. Yet this has been done both at Bitonto and at Bari. Yet perchance the improvers of modern times might retort on the original architects, and ask why, when they had made three apses at the east end, they presently built up a wall to hide them. This is the arrangement both at Bitonto and in the two great churches of Bari. The notion of Normans working in Italy would almost seem to have been to make an Italian front at one end, and something approaching to a Norman front at the other end. Thus the church of Bitonto has an excellent west front of Italian outline, with details more Italian than Norman, and with the characteristic round window evidently designed from the beginning, though the one which is actually there must be of later date. Also there either has been or has been meant to be a portico over the lower stage of the west front, a thoroughly Italian notion. But the east end takes almost the form of a Norman west front; a Norman founder, it would seem, was not happy unless he could somewhere or other get two towers with an ornamental wall between them. To this end the apses are sacrificed. Instead of the three curved projections which form the main features of so many Italian, German, and indeed Norman, east ends, the whole east end is flat. The side apses are disguised by towers, one only of which is carried up to any height, while the great apse is hidden by the wall between the towers. Herein is the difference between Bitonto and Trani. At Trani there are no eastern towers, and the apses, though of amazing external height and no less amazing slightness of projection, are still real apses with a real curve. At Bitonto no one could know from the outside that there were any apses at all. As the ordinary ranges of arcades and windows are thus made impossible, the architect, like an English architect some generations later, threw his strength into a single east window, and certainly made one as large and as rich as was possible before the invention of tracery. An elaborate round-headed opening is covered with rich devices, and has wonderful monsters to bear up its side-shafts. This too is to be seen at Trani, and we shall come again to other examples at Bari. There is something very strange in these attempts to reconcile the ideas of Normandy and of Italy in one building. But in these flat east ends the result is that we get something which is certainly neither Italian nor Norman, and which can hardly be approved according to any law of either reality or beauty.

The same spirit of compromise goes on in other parts. The endless columns of the under-church supply a rich study of capitals, largely of the grotesque kind. Men, monkeys, the original ram's horn, leaves, the Imperial eagle—better suited for the purpose than anything else—all do duty as volutes. The columns in the upper-church too give another rich collection of various kinds of human, animal, and vegetable forms. But here a soberer spirit reigns; though perhaps no one capital is strictly classical, yet the grotesque does not reign as it does below. Three arches from columns, a solid block, three more arches from columns, make up the nave. Over these Italian elements Norman taste set a triforium; modern taste has hidden the clerestory. Outside, the Italian has his way in the rich open arcades of the parapets and in the windows of various forms, filled, some of them, with that kind of pierced tracery which is neither Italian nor Norman, but distinctively Oriental, and which look as if they had come—as they possibly may have come—from a mosque.

Altogether there is something singularly interesting in this mixture of styles—more strictly this mixture of two varieties of the same style, for Italian and Norman Romanesque are after all members of one great artistic family. Nothing of the kind happened in Sicily, where the Norman kings simply set native craftsmen, Greek and Saracen, to build for them after their several native fashions. Here, in a land where Greek and Latin elements were striving for mastery, where the Saracen was a mere occasional visitor, the Norman brought in the ideas of his own land to make a new element. But, if nothing like this happened in Sicily, something a little like it did happen in England. There is no doubt that Norman architecture was influenced, though very slightly, by the earlier native style of England, a rude imitation of Italian models. That Norman architecture in Apulia should be far more deeply influenced by the Italian models themselves was but carrying out the same general process, as was only natural, in a far greater degree.

IX. BARI.

We are now at Barium, Bari, the original Bari of the West, as distinguished from the Bari, *Bar, Antibaris, Antivari,* which repeats its name on the opposite coast. There we can now again, as we could have done seventy years back at Cattaro, land at a Montenegrin haven. The distinction between the two bearers of the name of Bari implies an association which is not out of place. The historic interest of Bari gathers wholly round its connexion with the lands on the other side of Hadria. In earlier days the place has really no history whatever. Its most memorable day was when the powers of the Eastern and Western Empires—powers which perhaps never again worked in such harmony—were needed to dislodge a Saracen Sultan from its walls. "Emir," some one will say, not "Sultan," and certainly we are more used in Europe to Sultans of much later date than the days of Lewis the Second and Basil the First, Sultans coming from quite other lands than any that can have sent forth the Mussulman prince of Bari. But he is called Sultan as well as Emir by his one biographer, the Emperor Constantine, and we cannot appeal from those august pages which still form the best guide-book to the eastern shores of the Hadriatic. Anyhow, the Sultan of Bari was a philosopher; he never laughed, except once when he saw a wheel go round; for that reminded him of the ups and downs of his own fortunes. Then Bari passes to the rule of the Eastern Empire; instead of a Sultan it has a Katapan, representative of the Eastern Augustus in that Italian dominion which had become so small at the beginning of the ninth century, and which was so great again at its end. Threatened again at the beginning of the eleventh century by new Saracen invaders, it is guarded by the fleets of Venice, still the faithful vassal of Constantinople against a common enemy. Seventy years later the arms of Robert Wiscard added the capital of Byzantine Italy to his Norman dominion, and before the century was out, Pope Urban, the great stirrer of the West against the Mussulman East, chose Bari as the scene of the Council called to denounce at once the practical abuses of the Christian West and the dogmatic errors of the Christian East. Once more, in the next age, we find Bari looking across the sea to its old lord, and chastised by the Sicilian king for its disloyalty. Add that Bari, before all saints, still honours St. Nicolas of the Lykian Myra, and keeps his relics sacred, we are told, from Turkish desecration by the craft of merchants of her own city. Altogether Bari seems, at least in its history, as much Greek as Italian or Norman. It would seem neither unnatural nor unpleasant if Greek were still the tongue of the seafaring folk of Bari, much as a Norman in his own land often carries an air about him which would make Danish seem a much more natural speech for him than French.

But the great buildings of Bari belong to that mixed Norman and Italian style of which we have already seen something at Bitonto. The architectural attractions of the city are chiefly to be found in two great churches and one smaller one. The castle, standing by the sea, should have its landward side walked round, and the walk will reveal much of picturesque outline and a little of good detail. But it is the churches, above all the great abbey of St. Nicolas, which are the glory of Bari. They all lie in the old town by the sea, the old town of narrow and crooked streets, in which it does not much matter which way you go; you are sure to come either to the castle or to one of the churches before very long. Very different are things in the new town, which we may rejoice in as we look at it as a sign of Bari's abiding or renewed prosperity, but which can raise no feelings of pleasure on any other ground. Its streets, crossing each other at right angles, are indeed carefully dedicated to the worthies of Bari; but, unless we can always remember which of several perhaps not very familiar worthies watches over each of several angles which are exactly alike, it is easy to take a wrong turn and to put oneself under the care of Andrew of Bari when we ought rather to be commending ourselves to Robert. And under either protection we yearn in the wide straight streets for some physical shelter from the Apulian sun, and wonder why modern Rome, modern Athens, and modern Bari should have so much less common sense than Bologna, Padua, and Corfu had in days long past. Still, amid this rectangular labyrinth the sea is a help on one side, while on another the tall tower of the metropolitan church of St. Sabinus beckons us into the older streets, whose narrowness and crookedness at least supply shade. That tower, one of the tallest and stateliest of Italy, we naturally assume to be a detached campanile, without a fellow and standing apart from its confederate buildings, church and baptistery. So it doubtless would be in a purely Italian city; but here we are in the city where the Norman displaced the Greek. The two great churches of Bari, like that of Bitonto, have their towers wrought into the building in Norman fashion, and at the *duomo* the great round baptistery is also merged in the same mass with the church and its towers. Both of the great churches of Bari have east ends of the same kind as that at Bitonto; the apses are swallowed up; the place where the great apse should be is marked by a single splendid Romanesque window. The eastern towers of St. Nicolas have never been carried up; at St. Sabinus the southern one has perished, but the northern one still soars in all its majesty, thoroughly Italian in its conception, but rather to be called Norman in its detail. St. Nicolas has also another pair of unfinished towers at its west end, standing at once beyond the aisles as at Wells and Rouen, and in front of them as at Holyrood. They flank a grand Italian front which one would think would be finer without them. These western towers are absent in the metropolitan church; but that has a most perfect octagonal cupola over the crossing, the grouping of which with the two lofty eastern towers, if there was any point from which it could really be seen, must have been wonderful. Thus, in both churches, something of a German outline has either been consciously brought in or has been incidentally stumbled on. The four towers of St. Nicolas, the octagon and eastern tower of St. Sabinus, will easily find Rhenish fellows, though we should perhaps have to go as far as Angoulême for a single tower of equal majesty mourning over a vanished brother. In other points the external arrangements of the two great churches of Bari have much in common. The rose windows, the coupled windows, the blank arcades, are much the same in both. So is the choice of animal forms for the fanciful supports of columns. In most places the lion discharges that function—in a building designed by lions we should doubtless see something different. So we do here at Bari, where the solid forms of the *pachydermata* are, perhaps discreetly, preferred to the lighter *carnivora*. The elephant, we think, is to be found in both churches, and the huge earth-shaking beast is represented so as to remind us both of Pyrrhos and of Hannibal; some have the smaller ear of India, some the larger of Africa. The hippopotamus appears only in the west front of St. Nicolas. Had the daring shipfolk who bore away the saint's bones from Lykia made their way to the Nile also?

When we pass the threshold of the two buildings we see that their fate in modern times has been very different. St. Sabinus has suffered much as Bitonto has suffered. The upper part of the building is hidden in just the same fashion, and ugly tricks have been played with the columns and their capitals. St. Nicolas, on the other hand, has been left comparatively alone. The chief changes which it has undergone must have taken place not very long after the original building. The original plan was much the same as that of Bitonto—three arches from columns, a massive pier, then three more arches from columns. But this arrangement was disturbed at an early time by throwing three spanning arches across the nave. The effect is so striking that we can hardly regret their presence; but it is perfectly easy to see that they are insertions, and, though they are essentially of the same style, yet they differ in their details from the original columns. These last all approach more or less to the Corinthian type; in the under-church the patterns are more varied. Here are still the wonder-working relics of St. Nicolas, and the balsam or "manna" which flows from them may still be drunk. In the *duomo* the under-church has been restored out of all ancient character, but it still keeps an ancient Byzantine picture.

As so often happens, the secondary church of Bari altogether surpassed the mother church in historic fame and local honour. To ourselves the fact in its history which comes home most nearly is that it was here that Urban held his Council, here that Anselm, to the satisfaction of all Western minds, refuted the creed of the East, here that he interceded with the Pontiff and the assembled fathers on behalf of the king who had wronged him. Here too it was that the keen eye of English Eadmer spied out on the shoulders of the Archbishop of Beneventum the splendid cope which is no longer to be seen at Beneventum. Such little touches in those days often brought the ends of the world together in a way to which, in our days of more general intercourse, nothing answers. When French was the polite language alike at Dunfermline and at Jerusalem, when the Latin-speaking clerk was at home in any corner of the West, when the few men of the West who had learned Greek spoke it so that a Greek could understand them, when men passed to and fro between the civil services of England and Sicily, communication between distant parts of Europe was in some ways easier than it is now. Bari, one of the chief places for setting out on crusades, must for a long time have been a thoroughly cosmopolitan city. We do feel that the ends of the earth have combined to meet at Bari, when we find the place of honour in the church of St. Nicolas at Bari held by a princess of Bari, who became Queen of the greatest Slavonic kingdom. Emblematic figures of Bari and Poland support the tomb of Queen Bona, and her epitaph describes her husband Sigismund, the first of that name, as not only the mighty King of Poland, but Grand-Duke of Lithuania, Russia, Prussia, Mazovia, and Samogitia. Yet we might have lighted on Slavonic associations earlier on the road. There is a strange record of a Bulgarian settlement in the parts of Beneventum; but that would take us yet further afield: it was before Bulgarians became Slavonic. But what are we to say to the Samnite *Schiavia* which sheltered Anselm?

The journey is done—

"Brundisium longæ finis cartæque viæque."

Otranto lies yet further; but Otranto, yet more notably than Bari, comes within the Venetian *Notitia*. So does Brundisium, city of the stag's horn, of the haven so aptly called, if we only knew in what tongue it is that *Brentesium* has that meaning. But we are tempted to regret that Brindisi and not Otranto is the point for which Hadria has to be crossed. Brindisi has no moral claim. We cannot look thence, as we can from Otranto, upon the mountains of still enslaved Epeiros; no one is tempted even to dream that he looks on free Corfu or on the lesser satellite that stands in front as its outpost.